RESOURCING
CLASSROOM DRAMA: 5-8

Teresa Grainger & Mark Cremin

NATE

ACKNOWLEDGEMENTS

We would like to thank all the children and teachers who contributed to the creation of this book, through their involvement in these dramas. In particular Vivienne Resch, the headteacher of Slade School, Tonbridge, Wentworth School, Dartford, Hythe Infants, Folkestone, Belvedere Primary, Thamesmead, and Star Lane School, Newham. Also Ann Shreeve, NATE's Publications Officer for her tolerance, support, and advice, and Jo Bradbury our photographer. We are additionally indebted to the many teachers we have worked with us on in-service courses, and those who have welcomed us into their classrooms to teach their children. Finally, to our own children, Patrick and Lucy who also deserve our thanks and love, for the time they have missed us during the writing of this book.

PERMISSIONS

We are grateful to the following for permissions to reproduce illustrations:

A Dark, Dark Tale by Ruth Brown: Anderson Press
How The Birds Changed Their Feathers by Joanna Troutghton: Penguin UK
Peter and the Wolf by Ian Beck: Transworld Publishers
The Bakerloo Flea by Michael Rosen: Michael Rosen
Rama and the Demon King by Jessica Souhami: Francis Lincoln Ltd, 4 Torriano Mews,
   Torriano Avenue, London, NW5 2RU
The Lady of Shalott illustrated by Charles Keeping: B L Kearley Ltd

We are grateful to the following for permissions to reproduce text:

Through That Door, poem by John Cotton
The Bakerloo Flea, short story by Michael Rosen

Every effort has been made to trace the copyright holders of material included in this book. However, the authors and publisher offer their apologies if any material has been included without permission and will happily include appropriate acknowledgment in any future edition.

NATE 2001
Published by NATE, 50 Broadfield Road,
Sheffield, S8 0XJ
Tel: 0114 255 5419
Fax: 0114 255 5296

ISBN 0 901291 78 1

Designed, typeset and printed by
Quorn Selective Repro Limited, Loughborough, Leicestershire.

CONTENTS

imagining
and
believing

Introduction

'Keep quiet and don't move', Liam hissed in an urgent whisper, *'It's coming this way now.'* Someone called out, *'The dragon…!'* The children, huddled together in groups around the classroom, became silent and still. The air was full of expectation and tension. Their teacher, as narrator of the drama, eventually spoke: *'and so the intrepid explorers finally caught sight of the notorious creature they had been seeking. It stood before them in the clearing, its red eyes glinting in the sunlight, its ears pricking up as it looked and it listened. No one moved, no one spoke, but several felt their hearts beating faster. Then, with a sudden toss of its head, it turned and lumbered away. Was it satisfied…? Would it return…?'*

The class gathered spontaneously around the leader of the expedition, (their teacher in role), and told each other about the dragon. After some animated discussion, the explorers decided to draw diagrams of the creature in their log books. Some children, it turned out, had taken photographs so they produced them with labels illuminating the beast's physical features. These six-year-olds were engrossed in their drama, they were living imaginatively inside the fictional world they had created and were full of energy, ideas and commitment. Much later, having captured it for a zoo, they found it frail and feeble in its cage. An impassioned debate about their actions followed in an expedition meeting. *'We must admit we were wrong and let it go'*, Alistair insisted and many agreed with him, arguing against the captivity they had earlier imposed upon it. However, Ben, Morgan and others challenged this view,

'We can't go back to England with nothing.'
'We must take it back – no one will believe we saw it.'
'What will people think of us – that we failed?'

Classroom drama like this is imaginatively and intellectually demanding and holds considerable potential for learning. It involves making and shaping new worlds, investigating issues in them and returning to the real world with more understanding and insight. In this book we focus throughout on such drama, rather than on theatre, performance skills or role play areas. Whilst these are obviously valuable and related to whole class improvisational drama, our explicit intention is to profile classroom drama and to provide teachers with a better grasp of it in practice. In classroom drama, learners create and experience a living narrative and examine it from within. Their teacher, often in role, accompanies the class on this journey and uses a range of other drama conventions to investigate the themes, characters, motives or issues in the evolving tale. Reflecting upon these themes and finding parallels in real life is a significant part of the drama and heightens its relevance to the children.

We aim to support teachers in planning and resourcing classroom drama so Part One provides a range of lessons all of which have been taught to primary children. We hope teachers will make use of these example lessons and gradually become more confident in planning their own work and selecting appropriate resources to prompt dramatic investigations. The pressures of recent years have reduced the opportunity for creative activity in school, yet drama is a powerful and motivating activity: drama is imagination in action.

There are a wide range of resources which can prompt classroom drama, including fiction and poetry, music and art, faith tales and history, science and geography and even objects, as well as the children's own lives. We've tried to reflect this diversity in the resource chapters and show how drama can be integrated into cross-curricular work and operate as an effective learning strategy. Whilst this book does not offer a sequential programme of drama sessions, the chapters in Part One do reflect a gradual increase in complexity and demand. The sessions are offered as stepping stones to increase confidence and competence in classroom drama, and as jumping off points/resource banks for planning future dramas. Each of the resource chapters identifies the teaching objectives and learning areas (the latter are italicised), and provides a guiding framework for drama which involves: First Encounters: Creating the Drama Context, Conflicts and Tensions: Developing the Drama, and Resolutions: Drawing the Drama Together. Extension activities and ideas for resourcing further dramas from the named resources are also offered.

Depending on the time available and the children's experience of drama, you may find several of the dramas described could be spread over a number of sessions. If their initial encounter with the theme really hooks the children's interest, they will happily revisit the same drama with enthusiasm and commitment. But do be selective in deciding upon the suggestions you wish to use from each chapter, much will depend upon the children's responses and interest. Avoiding the children's suggestions and responses in order to follow the plan may mean that real opportunities for relevant learning are missed. A professional balance between following the teaching objectives and the children's interests is always required.

In Part Two, issues around organising, teaching and assessing classroom drama are discussed. *Planning* classroom drama is examined in some detail to support the teacher in identifying the key elements of drama: people, place and predicament, which create a secure structure for the session. *Assessing* classroom drama is addressed, through considering the major areas of learning in drama, including: the imagination, personal and social skills, drama processes, language, reflection and the content area of the drama. Ways of recording children's development are also noted. *Managing* the eager enthusiasm of young learners during the drama session is also discussed and a number of questions we've been asked repeatedly, are responded to in some detail. Since drama is placed within English in the National Curriculum, we have devoted one short chapter to *Drama and Literacy Time*, noting how drama conventions can be harnessed for shared reading or as a precursor to shared writing. However, we argue that merely employing a single drama convention for literacy purposes is not engaging in full classroom drama. When a range of conventions are employed to investigate a text, or are used to devise alternative actions and solutions, there is the possibility of co-authoring a new and living fiction. Different *Drama Conventions* are focused upon in each chapter and are examined further in the last chapter, which seeks to explain the nature and function of the different conventions. Many of these conventions are used repeatedly, because of their power to support the development of drama. In particular, the teacher in role and the teacher using narration, are highlighted as strategies we recommend from the outset of teaching classroom drama.

Classroom drama represents much more than a way of responding to the statutory orders for English. It offers children the chance to create and inhabit imaginary worlds together, and to learn from living in drama time with their teacher. It is a motivating and engaging process, a refreshing and empowering act of creativity.

**feeling
and
sharing**

Hey diddle diddle, the cat and the fiddle,

The cow jumped over the moon.

The little dog laughed to see such fun,

And the dish ran away with the spoon.

Chapter 1

A NURSERY RHYME: HEY DIDDLE DIDDLE

Introduction

This traditional nursery rhyme celebrates an 'upside down' world in which the normal rules or expectations of existence are flouted, with animals and everyday objects being given human abilities. Children find nursery rhymes fun, not only because of their rhyme and repetition, but also because they undermine the real and predominantly adult controlled world and create an alternative world of nonsense and pleasure.

This drama has two parts. The first offers the opportunity to investigate how the physical world of the child, in particular their home, is ordered, by visiting a topsy turvy upside down world and finding a Crooked House in which everything is out of its place, or literally upside down. The children are invited to sort out the mess and to give it some order. In the second part they revisit the Topsy Turvy World, find another house of their description and choice, and respond to the new predicament it presents.

The drama convention highlighted in the chapter is **teacher in role**, an indispensable tool in early years drama, which allows the teacher to work alongside the children, join them imaginatively and challenge them in their roles. Another convention used extensively is **whole class improvisation** in which the children make the drama happen by living in the Topsy Turvy World with their teacher and responding to each other spontaneously.

Avoiding the children's suggestions and responses in order to follow the plan may mean that real opportunities for relevant learning are missed. A professional balance between teaching objectives and children's interests is always required.

Teaching Objectives and Learning Areas

- Enter an imaginary world *(the imagination)*
- Distinguish between order and disorder *(the content of the drama)*
- Take part in whole class improvisation *(the drama processes)*.

Prior Experience and Materials

- Knowledge of nursery rhymes.
- A single item such as a crown, handbag or pinafore to indicate the teacher is in role.
- Pencil and paper for each child.

First Encounters: Creating the Drama Context

LOOKING THROUGH THE MAGIC WINDOW

- Chant some nursery rhymes together and comment on how many are 'topsy turvy', and nonsensical. Ask the class if they know other such rhymes.
- Share some more and stop at Hey Diddle Diddle and repeat it a couple of times together.

- Invite the children enthusiastically to make their own Topsy Turvy World of nursery rhymes.

- Tell them you that you have a magic finger and quite slowly and deliberately draw a large window in the air.

- Name the things you can see through the magic window and ask the children what they can see in the Topsy Turvy, Upside Down World? Generate ideas together, e.g. purple clouds, orange grass, dinosaurs flying by, an egg sitting on a wall, cows jumping over the moon and so on. Accept all their ideas but encourage the children to describe imaginary things and not to name the nearby objects they see.

ENTERING THE TOPSY TURVY WORLD

- Suggest you hold hands and go together through the window to investigate this Upside Down World.

- Mime opening the window and lead the class into this imaginary Topsy Turvy World of Nursery Rhymes. Use your voice to convey a sense of anticipation and excitement.

- Stop once everyone is through. Ask the children to explore the place in pairs and find any strange things which break the laws of nature, e.g. a hedgehog riding a bicycle or characters from Nursery Rhymes.

- Freeze everyone into statues and visit several children enquiring about what they have seen and asking a few probing questions.

Conflicts and Tensions: Developing the Drama

WHOSE HOME IS THIS?

- Tell the children that you have seen a funny Crooked House and suggest that you all go and look at it. Ask the class to hold hands, make a circle around the house and peer in through the windows.

- Observe that the place is all 'higgledy piggledy' with all sorts of things in the wrong places, give them some examples e.g. there's a hat in the sink and a clock in the bath, a saucepan hanging from a coat-peg and so on. Ask them to share what they can see which is in the wrong place with their neighbour. Then decide with the children about where some of these objects should be kept, and ponder on whose house this might be.

Jodie (aged 5)

- Tell the children you'd like to pretend to be someone else in the story they are making, and ask them if that is all right? If they agree, tell them you're going to walk away from them and when you return you will pretend to be the person who lives in the house.

- In role as the character (e.g. The Queen of Hearts, Little Miss Muffet, the White Queen from Alice, or Mr Muddle), walk towards your home, wearing a single appropriate item e.g. a crown, a pinafore etc.

- Narrate your own return '*Just as the children were wondering who lived there, back came The Queen of Hearts, she'd been shopping and was in a terrible dither*' and come across the children with surprise, and behave somewhat helplessly. You have a friend Wee Willie Winkie who is coming to have tea, but the house is in such a mess, and Wee Willie Winkie may not be able to find anywhere to sit, everywhere is such a muddle and you just don't know what to do. Can they suggest anything?

- If they don't spontaneously offer to help, ask them directly, and check how long they can stay and whether they know where to put things? Explain how very grateful you'd be if they could help you.

ORGANISING THE HOUSE

- Open the imaginary front door, and welcome them into your home, give them permission and encouragement to clear up any room and put things back in their right place.

- Join the class in improvising the return of items to their rightful places and ask various individuals what they are putting back and where, thanking them individually. As the muddle is sorted, find some missing items like a key or an old photograph and show these to your helpers. Have they found other more precious items in the wrong place?

- In role, pass out paper and ask the children to draw a plan of your house to show you the furniture and other items in their correct place. This will help you keep your house tidy and organised, when they've gone.

- Collect their drawings, thank them for their help and suggest they might come and visit you again.

Resolutions: Drawing the Drama Together

RETURNING SAFELY HOME

- Take off your crown/pinafore and then as their class teacher draw the magic window and step back through it into the classroom with the children.

- Comment reflectively about your trip to the Topsy Turvy World of Nursery Rhymes. Prompt discussion: what was their favourite part of the adventure, what did they find out about the Queen of Hearts, when have they experienced a mess like that, why is it helpful to be organised...?

REVISITING THE TOPSY TURVY WORLD (SESSION 2)

- Invite the class to make a return visit, draw the magic window and ask them to tell you what they see, and suggest that you all go and visit the world.

- Step through the window and meet a problem, the blue mud is very sticky, adhesive even – how can they cope with it?

- Narrate your journey through the land, perhaps pausing to let them rest, sit down and observe. Point out to them a house in a clearing in a wood. Ponder about what it is made from, who might live in it? Listen to all their suggestions e.g. a house of sweets, a fairy palace, a little cottage, a wizard's home. Decide with them which type of house it will be in the drama you are creating.

Sam (aged 5)

11

- Together go to the house and see what happens – many classes will create their own predicament e.g. by eating the sweets or seeing the three bears.
- Enter in role as the owner, share your concern that your house needs renovating e.g. the sweets have been nibbled, the place needs redecorating. You want to sell, can they help you make it more desirable?
- Improvise the renovation process together.
- Draw pictures of the house for the estate agent's window.
- Return home via the magic window, discuss the visit and make connections between their life experience and the fictional adventure.

Extension Activities
- Make a simple class book of the story (in the shape of a house).
- Write/receive letters or postcards from the Queen of Hearts/the character they met.
- Storyboard the adventure.

Resourcing Further Drama from Nursery Rhymes

Nursery rhymes offer alternative worlds for dramatic investigation. In visiting these worlds children can meet the characters, share their problems and create new ones to be solved. The simple structure and basic nature of the narratives within them, make them ideal resources for drama sessions in the early years. Nursery rhymes can be used in the following ways.

1   **Selecting Rhymes to Develop and Investigate**
     Many rhymes have predicaments or themes which can be examined. The rhyme can be chanted and then different strategies used to enter the world, for example stepping through the magic window, the invisible door or creating a class spell or chant which transports the children to a different kingdom. Rhymes which have been used include:

     Little Boy Blue:
     (Sheep and cattle round up – ruined crops – irate farmers)

     The Queen of Hearts:
     (A royal garden party – stolen tarts – finding the culprit)

     There Was an Old Woman who Lived in a Shoe:
     (She needs help – advice about feeding large families and disciplining wild children.)

     Simple Simon:
     (He's hungry – how can he be helped to earn money – who might he share his pies with?)

2   **Using Retold Versions of Nursery Rhymes**
     Some new versions of old nursery rhymes develop the original by extending the text with new adventures or creating a modern alternative rhyme based on the structure of the old. These can be used as a structure to guide the drama, since they offer an explicit framework for investigation whilst also highlighting variation. In addition, such written texts can be used for closer study in literacy time. Examples of these include:

     Emma Chichester Clark (1997) *Little Miss Muffet Counts to Ten*, Anderson Press (Big Book).
     Sarah Hayes (1987) *The True Story of Humpty Dumpty*, Walker.
     Miko Imai (1994) *Little Lumpty*, Walker.
     Jan Ormerod (1996) *Ms Macdonald Had a Class*, Red Fox.
     Maureen Roffey and Bernard Lodge (1997) *The Grand Old Duke of York*, Bodley Head.

Chapter 2

A PICTURE: A DARK DARK PLACE

Introduction

This drama was developed from the picture of a gloomy mansion in Ruth Brown's *A Dark Dark Tale*. In the text, a cat goes exploring across a dark dark moor, finds a dark dark house, a dark dark door, some dark dark stairs, a dark dark passageway, a dark dark room, a dark dark cupboard, a dark dark corner and eventually… a mouse! All that was used to plan the drama was a picture of the house, which generated a sense of place and a possible predicament: a power cut! The picture was only used as a planning tool and was not shown to the children, although in other drama sessions based on a visual resource, children may begin by examining the picture and generating ideas from it for their drama.

In this drama, the class receive an invitation to join Baron Blessing for tea at his castle, they pack and find a way to travel there, but when they arrive, the castle is in darkness. Uncertain and outside in the cold, they try to cheer themselves up, but are later found by his housekeeper who explains there is a power cut and takes them inside. A grand tea is served in the Banqueting Hall and later a tour of the castle involves unexpected events before they return home safely.

The drama convention highlighted in this chapter is **freeze frame**, in which the children create corporate still pictures of events. **Teacher in role** is also fully used, with the teacher adopting three different roles in this drama, as narrator, as the Baron and as the housekeeper.

Avoiding the children's suggestions and responses in order to follow the plan may mean that real opportunities for relevant learning are missed. A professional balance between teaching objectives and children's interests is always required.

Teaching Objectives and Learning Areas

- Accept their teacher in a variety of roles *(the drama processes)*
- Tolerate the uncertainty of problematic situations *(personal and social skills)*
- Use language to conjecture, suggest and predict *(language)*.

Prior Experience and Materials

- No experience is necessary, although a focus on castles or work in science on dark and light would support the drama
- Plain wall lining paper or several A3 sheets joined together to create a long baronial table and pencils
- A hurricane lamp or torch
- A diagram of the interior of a house (e.g. from an estate agent or a stately home leaflet).

First Encounters: Creating the Drama Context

THE INVITATION

- Prior to the drama, privately arrange with a child that you are expecting an imaginary telephone call at some point during the coming class discussion: can they look after the 'phone', and tell you when it rings. But go on to say that you will look at them very pointedly when you wish this to happen, and that it won't be straight away.

- Gather the children together on the carpet and ask them about interesting places which they have visited. Have they been to the sea, to museums, to caves, a funfair or a castle? Discuss the places they mention and let them share their experiences of these places with one another.

- When the 'phone' rings, answer it and hold a one sided conversation with a Baron Blessing. Break off, holding your hand over a make believe mouthpiece and tell the children he's invited you all to a tea party in his manor house. Ask them if they would like to go?

- Continue this three way conversation asking the class various questions from the Baron e.g. *he wants to know what you would like for a special tea?* Convey their replies to the Baron and answer them in kind e.g. *he doesn't think MacDonalds delivers out into the country, but he wondered if you'd like strawberries with your ice cream?* Finally, tell the Baron everyone will be getting ready to leave immediately and you'll see him within the hour, and put the phone down.

- Share your excitement at the trip and ask the children to start getting changed for this special party at Baron Blessing's manor house. As they begin to mime this, move around and ask them what they are putting on.

- Stop them and prompt the children to pack a bag each, make suggestions e.g. are they taking precious toys or photos of their family to show the Baron? Are they taking a book for the journey or a snack? This time 'freeze' the children in mid action and move around asking individuals to tell the class what they have packed, probe a little and comment, e.g. why are you taking your camera? Is your dog good at travelling? I hope he doesn't get car sick.

A TRANSPORT PROBLEM

- Suggest you leave for the manor house, and then suddenly realise you have not thought of how you are all to get there! Sit the children down, apologise, and ask them how they might solve this transport problem. Discuss options, agree to try one and give the 'phone' to a volunteer to ring and see if a coach can be booked, or whether there is a train station nearby.

- Listen to, and accept the child's conversation with the transport company. Children will rarely say the coaches are all booked since they are keen to make the drama happen. If they do, however, try another form of transport.

- Narrate the class boarding onto whatever transport is chosen, you might lay out the appropriate seating arrangements with chairs if there is room. If not, indicate a shape with your hands.

- Ask the class to sit still while you take a souvenir photograph of them ready to travel, request quiet and smiles. Click your imaginary camera. This is, in effect, a whole class freeze frame which also serves as a control mechanism as it encourages them to settle down as you take the drama further.

Conflicts and Tensions: Developing the Drama

THE MANOR HOUSE IS IN DARKNESS

- Narrate the journey very briefly and suggest that as they travelled some children were thinking about the special tea which they'd requested: the iced buns, sausages on sticks and

In the wood there was
a dark, dark house.

tiny chocolate Teletubbies… (try to use the food items which the children suggested earlier so you are telling their tale; including their ideas and building upon them). Others were wondering what the manor house would be like inside, the portraits, chandeliers, beams, stag horns, armour from the past and so on.

- As teacher, announce your arrival, let the class off the coach, and point out that the castle has no lights on. You're puzzled, the Baron couldn't be out, could he? Didn't he say the tea party today was at 4 o'clock?

- Ask the class what they think you should do? In pairs or threes let them improvise their suggestions, which might include ringing the bell, knocking on the door, calling out, ringing from a mobile phone and so on.

- As narrator, comment that none of the ideas produced any response from within the manor house. If a child says he thinks he can see the Baron at a window, agree it might have been him, but remain disappointed he still hasn't come. If inappropriate suggestions occur appeal to the class's sense of morals e.g. do you really think we should break in?

- Through narration observe that it has begun to rain, so ask the children where they might shelter? Be led by the children now and crouch together in the old garage, shelter under the trees or in a barn, whatever they suggest.

- Shift the drama on by sharing your impatience and irritation at being stuck out in the cold and wet e.g. *What can we do? I'm cold and hungry and fed up!* Let suggestions for the next move come from the children, they will think quickly in their desire to solve the problem and make the best of the situation. Try out their suggestions e.g. shout out together, peer in the windows with a torch, write a note to put through the letter box. They may suggest you all sing songs, tell jokes to cheer each other up, or eat the snacks packed into their bags.

- Move away from the class as they are engaged in one of these activities, pick up your hurricane lamp, or torch, and narrate your entrance as the Baron's housekeeper e.g. *Just as the children were thinking they'd never get into the castle, a stout lady in a raincoat, who was carrying a hurricane lamp came hurrying towards them 'Aah, my dears, are you the children from St Joseph's who the Baron invited for tea?'* Talk to them, ask them how long they've been waiting and apologise, explaining that a recent electric power cut meant you didn't hear the bell ringing and so forth.

INSIDE AT LAST

- Welcome them in and suggest they take their wet coats off and hang them up. Explain that you're very behind with the tea now that all the electric power has gone and you need their help. Can they see anything in the kitchen which won't work because there's no electricity?

- Take a note book and list the items they find, or give out paper and pencils and ask the children to make lists. Explain that when the manor was first built there was no electricity, and people managed then, so there must be ways of coping. With a few items discuss alternatives e.g. if the toaster won't work, what can we do? This could be undertaken in pairs, small groups or as a class.

- Still in role as the housekeeper, thank them for their ideas and reassure them that some of the tea is already made. Take them through to the Banqueting Hall. Unroll the long strip of lining paper, put out the pencils and ask them formally to take their seats at the baronial dining table opposite one another. Describe the sumptuous banquet laid before them, the linen cloth, the fine china, the candelabra and the delicious (cold) feast which has been prepared. Encourage them to draw the plates of delicacies they can see in front of them upon the lining paper.

- Whilst they're drawing, invite some children to help you make some drinks or additional food and take it around.

- Announce their host's arrival and in role as the Baron, take your seat at the head of the table and welcome them formally to your manor house. Thank them for their patience and suggest that after tea they might like a tour of the manor, or is their coach waiting to return them to school? With less experienced and younger classes this may conclude the session, with the option of visiting again another week for a guided tour. If you wish to conclude here, move to Resolutions: Drawing the Drama Together.

STRANGE AND UNUSUAL HAPPENINGS

- As the Baron, show the children an interior diagram of your home, share a little history of the place and invite requests to explore various rooms.

- Take them to a room e.g. the baronial bedchamber, describe a little of it and its purpose in the past. Let them have a look around and then stop them, asking what they've found of interest e.g. portraits, antique furniture, suits of armour, silver pots. Add some embellishments e.g. you believe there might be treasure hidden in the house from years ago, or you were once told there were secret panels, but you don't know where.

- As storyteller, narrate that when the Baron was called to the phone, the children carried on exploring and that was when something surprising happened. Ask the children to make freeze frames of what happened, in groups or as a whole class. Ideas have included: exploring a secret passage; something/someone walking mournfully by; a knight in armour coming to life; a secret panel opening; ghostly figures appearing; bats in the tower flapping about; a portrait talking and so on.

- Return as the Baron and check if everything is all right, listen to their descriptions and either confirm that such things have happened before or justify the events/sightings with a logical explanation. These happenings could be the basis for further drama.

Resolutions: Drawing the Drama Together

HEADING HOME EXHAUSTED

- In role as the Baron or the housekeeper, hear the coach's horn beeping, and announce it's time for them to leave, thank them for coming and escort them onto their transport home.
- Narrate their return home in tired and reflective mood, e.g. the children slept soundly in their seats on the coach remembering that afternoon, the waiting outside, the big old kitchen, the wonderful tea in the banqueting hall. They wondered had they really heard someone wailing in another room? In effect you revisit their ideas and the drama whilst they repose on the coach.
- In review time, discuss with the class which part of the afternoon's outing they enjoyed most, what surprised them, what didn't they like, what did they think of the Baron and so forth.

Extension Activities

- Write thank you letters or cards to the Baron.
- On the tape recorder, let pairs of children role-play the class teacher telling the headteacher about the outing.
- Draw and label a picture of one room in the Baron's manor house.
- Return to Baron Blessing's home weeks later and travel in his special time machine into the past to examine living in the manor house without electricity.
- Use Ruth Brown's *A Dark Dark Tale* for literacy work and explain to the children where you got the idea for their drama. Discuss connections and differences.

Resourcing Further Drama from Pictures

A variety of visual artwork can be used to resource drama: evocative and dramatic portrayals in picture books, reproductions of famous artist's work, photographs of scenes/people, photo stories as well as cartoons in comics. All of these imply a story or an event. Pictures which provide a sense of place and the people as well as the predicament offer rich opportunies for drama. However, visuals can also be used to provide just one of these dimensions, whilst the remainder are planned by the teacher and/or the class. In the following examples the visual is offered to the children, but teachers can also use them separately for prior planning.

1   **Focus on the People**

    Examine a picture closely with the class (in groups or as a whole) and generate ideas about the people portrayed. Who are they, what are they doing there, what's their relationship to one another? What's just happened? Use their ideas to bring the people to life in an improvisation or a freeze frame – what are they thinking? Through the drama build a story with the class around the characters about whom little is known. Examples which have been used include:

    Sarah Hayes and Caroline Binch (1996) *Down by the River,* Heinemann.
    Susan Hill and Angela Barrett (1993) *Beware, Beware,* Walker.
    Millais (1856) *The Blind Girl,* City Museum and Art Gallery, Birmingham.
    Jane Northway (1997) *Lucy's Quarrel,* Hippo.

2   **Focus on the Place**

    Show the children a single picture which evokes a clear sense of place. Together, list a number of people (characters) who might visit that place (setting) and then create freeze frames of a problem (narrative action) which they might encounter. The class could vote to agree the characters and then establish a drama to explore particular learning areas emerging from this. Examples include:

Jex Alborough (1992) *Where's My Teddy?,* Walker.
Mike Haddon and Christian Birmingham (1996) *The Sea of Tranquility,* Harper Collins.
Kathy Henderson and Patrick Bension (1995) *The Little Boat,* Walker.
Dyan Sheldon and Gary Blythe (1993) *The Garden,* Random House.
Lowry and Brueghel paintings provide a sense of place, a village community and weather conditions, e.g. *The Return of the Hunters* (1565) P Brueghel.

3   Focus on People, Place and Predicament

Show the class the front cover or a single inner picture of an unknown text or painting. The picture will provide some information regarding the people, the place and the predicaments within the text. Using various drama techniques create a story drama based on this limited information. Examples include:

Chris Van Allsburg (1984) *The Mysteries of Harris Burdick,* Houghton Mifflin Co.
Ian Beck (1989) *The Teddy Robber,* Picture Corgi.
Berlie Doherty and Christian Birmingham (1996) *The Magical Bicycle,* Picture Lions.
Millais (1870) *A Flood,* City Art Gallery, Manchester.

4   Share the Initial Pictures in a Visual Text, stopping at the Predicament

Give the children photocopies of the first few visuals in an unknown picture book or cartoon, one at a time. Use these in small groups to generate possibilities, share connections, and make meaning out of the unfolding text together. At a predicament in the text, offer no more visuals but step into the world of drama and use techniques to flashback, flash forward and create possible resolutions. Examples include:

Allan Ahlberg and Andre Amstutz (1998) *Monkey Do!,* Walker

A young monkey borrows the zookeeper's keys and releases himself, he explores the zoo but it isn't all plain sailing…

John Burningham (1996) *Cloudland,* Jonathan Cape

Albert, climbing with his parents, falls off a mountain and is saved by the Cloud Children…

Philippe Dupasquier (1992) *Follow that Chimp,* Walker

A chimp escapes from the zoo to follow a friendly young visitor and is pursued himself by his relentless captors, through the traffic, on a train, a boat and so on…

Chris Wright (1991) *When the World Sleeps,* Red Fox

One night the moon falls out of the sky, one boy happens to see this, do others? What can be done… ?

Chapter 3

A POEM:
THROUGH THAT DOOR, BY JOHN COTTON

Through that door
Is a garden with a wall,
The red brick crumbling,
The lupins growing tall,
Where the lawn is like a carpet
Spread for you,
And it's all as tranquil
As you never knew.

Through that door
Is the great ocean-sea
Which heaves and rolls
To eternity,
With its islands and promontories
Waiting for you
To explore and discover
In that vastness of blue.

Through that door
Is your secret room
Where the window lets in
The light of the moon,
With its mysteries and magic
Where you can find
Thrills and excitements
Of every kind.

Through that door
Are the mountains and the moors
And the rivers and the forests
Of the great outdoors,
All the plains and the ice-caps
And lakes as blue as sky
For all those creatures
That walk or swim or fly.

Through that door
Is the city of the mind
Where you can imagine
What you'll find.
You can make of that city
What you want it to,
And if you choose to share it,
Then it could come true.

John Cotton

Introduction

Each of the verses of this evocative poem could be the source of a drama session; for they each refer to a different real or imaginary place. These clearly defined places offer the teacher the opportunity to identify the people who live or travel there, and a chance to discover and investigate the situations they encounter. The drama session detailed here, is planned around verse two; the 'great ocean-sea' which the children can read and then journey across in their drama, creating life on board a ship.

The drama involves the teacher in role as the Captain who recruits the class as sailors onto the ship. On board 'The Enterprise' jobs are shared, stowaways discovered and land is sighted. On the Island of Taste, the sailors experience new flavours and cook more familiar ones in a banquet on the beach, whilst on the Island of Touch they are given some 'boxes of surprises'. They travel around the other islands each one of which is based upon experience of the senses and return home with many a tale to tell. You and the class could visit one island, or you could visit each in turn in an extended session, or a series of sessions, by chanting a verse as a magical incantation, or using the magic mirror to step in and out of drama time.

A range of drama conventions are employed, but **mime** is highlighted, sometimes this is prompted by **the teacher as storyteller**, (who paints word and action pictures which the children interpret in their own manner), whilst sometimes they mime without this support. The convention of teacher as storyteller weaves the adventure together, integrating the children's ideas into a developing narrative. Ceremony is also used, which is a convention that marks out significant events, in this case a celebratory meal.

Avoiding the children's suggestions and responses in order to follow the plan may mean that real opportunities for relevant learning are missed. A professional balance between teaching objectives and children's interests is always required.

Teaching Objectives and Learning Areas

- Use, recognise, and discuss the senses (*the content of the drama*)
- Generate appropriate ideas for each of the islands visited (*the imagination*)
- Respect others' ideas and suggestions (*personal and social skills*).

Prior Experience and Materials

- A simultaneous focus on ships/seafarers, and the senses would support the drama but is not necessary
- Pencil and paper for menu making
- An enlarged copy of the poem (optional)
- Two special boxes to contain treasure
- Chalked/taped shape of the ship on the floor.

First Encounters: Creating the Drama Context

PREPARING FOR THE VOYAGE ON THE GREAT OCEAN SEA

- Read the poem to the class a couple of times, perhaps displaying an enlarged copy, which allows shared re-reading of verse two. Discuss their experience of the sea and boats.
- Introduce yourself as the Captain of a sailing-ship, invite them to sail with you on a voyage of discovery. You need sailors on board 'The Enterprise' to cross the 'great ocean sea which heaves and rolls to eternity' and find new lands.
- Suggest everyone packs a small kit bag for the trip, food will be provided, but what other items might sailors need? Allow a little time for packing and then stop the class and ask a few children what they are taking with them.
- Draw an imaginary magic mirror in the air, which, if they wink as they step through, will transport them down to the sea. As they follow you through the mirror and around the classroom, begin the tale of how the young sailors with their kit bags on their backs are led by Captain… (your name), down to the ship moored at the harbour-side. Paint a brief word picture of the ship.
- Show the children the plan of the ship, which you have chalked/taped on the floor, and as Captain welcome them aboard. Shake hands with some of the sailors, greet others verbally as old ship-mates from previous voyages, remind all of them of the purpose of this trip: to discover new islands in the vast and unexplored parts of the ocean.
- As the Captain run through with your crew, all the jobs to be done on board, record their suggestions and add your own.
- Narrate setting sail from the harbour and then ask the children to choose a job and do it. Move round the class talking about the work they are improvising. You may wish to stop the class and watch a number of sailors at work, and allow other members of the class to ask questions about what they are doing: Is that a heavy anchor? What are you cooking for tea? What is the design upon the flag you are hoisting?
- Ask them to continue with their jobs and encourage them to talk to each other as they work. During this, quietly ask three children, and/or a learning support assistant, to join you and invite them to be stowaways. In role as Captain, interrupt the class improvisation with the announcement that you've found some stowaways. Can they all gather round, what should we do? This whole class meeting will need to find out more about the stowaways in order to decide what action to take. Where did they come from? Who are they? Could they earn their keep?

Conflicts and Tensions: Developing the Drama

THE ISLAND OF TASTES

- As storyteller, narrate the incident about the stowaways and what was decided about them. Continue by describing the long days at sea: the terrible winds, the strange stars that glowed at night, the endless motion of the ocean, and recount their first sight of land. Describe the red glow coming from the island, which the sailors gradually realised, came from a multitude of campfires on a promontory.

- Narrate their landing, then step into role as the Head Chef on this the Island of Taste and welcome them. Tell them their arrival has been long awaited, and many unusual tastes and novel menus are planned for their delectation. Offer a few sailors a spoonful of their favourite foods from a large cooking pot, asking them what flavours they taste?

- Invite the sailors to make a circle around your pot (or in small groups around different cooking pots) and offer each child a 'spoon' to dip carefully into the pot, what tastes do they find? Dip in yourself and name some ordinary flavours: ketchup and sausages, then some extraordinary flavours: happiness and fear, and then the absurd: purple bananas or cucumber chocolate. Let them suggest tastes and share their ideas.

- As Head Chef, ask them about the food they eat on board their ship and at home. Express surprise and ignorance at some items and ask them to tell you more e.g. you've never heard of spaghetti, it sounds like worms, you have never tried a milkshake and so on.

- Request that they create a menu for a special celebration, with a main meal, pudding and a drink, for the cooks on the island, who always like to try different tastes. Provide paper and pencils and still in role, get pairs or small groups to plan, record, and decorate their menus. Narrate the start of a splendid banquet on the beach.

Jade and Lucy (aged 5)

- Ritualise the banquet altogether; slowly improvise the serving, tasting and toasting, perhaps with a speech from you as the Captain in praise of the food, and words from anyone else who wishes to speak. Children may wish to read their menus. The children could split into two groups with half of them in role as the local chefs, and half as sailors serving food on silver platters and pouring drinks.

- As storyteller, narrate the sailors clearing up their cooking. Encourage the class to mime loading the boat with boxes of new foods they have been given, thanking their hosts, and finally retiring to their bunks exhausted. The first drama session could close here, with the teacher re-reading the verse and drawing the magic mirror to return home.

TRAVELLING AROUND THE ISLANDS OF THE SENSES (SESSION TWO)

- In starting another session, recap their journey on board 'The Enterprise', and wink your way through the magic mirror onto the ship, chanting the verse as you go.

- Narrate that some months later the sailors on board ship discovered the surprising Island of Sight, where everything looked quite different. Ask them to make a freeze frame (whole class or group) of the sailors discovering intriguing flora and fauna on the island. What have they found? There is a possibility here of creating entries in the ship's log about their discoveries on the island.

- Narrate that the voyage of discovery continued, and one moonlit night when the sea was very calm and most of the crew were below deck almost asleep, they were aroused by a mixture of perfumes and aromas filling the air, some of which were wonderful and some revolting: they were passing the Island of Smell. The sailors drew in their breath and were reminded of the different smells of home. Pause to linger on this moment, and briefly let them share some of their memories and evocations.

- Tell the story of how they stumbled upon the Island of Touch when looking for fresh water. Everything they picked up or brushed against had a particularly interesting texture and the people who lived upon that island gave the sailors a precious gift of surprises: two locked boxes. Tell them that the next morning the Captain called a meeting to ceremoniously open the surprise boxes.

- In role as the Captain, invite the sailors to sit in a circle, and collect your real boxes. Carefully open these, taking out an imaginary object from each box and pretend to feel it in some way. You can accompany this with a description e.g. this is something smooth to touch: a mermaid's scarf, or this is something sharp to touch: a shark's tooth. Pass the boxes round the circle in opposite directions and encourage the children to take turns at opening a box, finding an object and describing its texture and its nature.

- As storyteller, narrate that the sailors had only one island left to discover and one night as they slept they heard… what was it… what could it be…? Was their boat nearing the Island of Sound? Who or what could be making those strange sounds in the night?

- Ask the children to decide on the source of the sound in groups and to create the noise too. Examples have included a strange sea monster, an ice machine, mermaids singing, a shark orchestra, ghosts of dead sailors and a family of ichthyosaurs. Listen to each one.

Resolutions: Drawing the Drama Together

RETURNING TO THE HARBOUR WITH MANY A STRANGE TALE TO TELL

- Gather the sailors in the boat again and retell the events of the night before including their ideas, 'Some sailors had heard ghosts wailing, while others had heard…' Finally narrate 'The Enterprise's' return home.

- Draw the magic mirror in the air again and as the class teacher open it from your side and welcome them back. Ask them about their journey. What foods or treasures have they bought home? Through discussion help them reflect upon their adventures and in particular focus on the senses.

- Ask them individually or in small groups to draw a map of their journey and the islands they visited when they went 'through that door to the great ocean sea'.

- While they are drawing re-read the verse and/or related poems about sea travel.

Extension Activities

- Read *Sleeping Nannah* by Kevin Crossley Holland, illustrated by P. Melynyczuk (1989) Orchard. You could use it as a text for literacy work and seek parallels and differences with their journey.

- Make the role-play area into 'The Enterprise'. Put in literacy materials such as the Captain's Log, maps, menus, food supplies, radio transmitters, cameras, reference books and so on and encourage groups to share their adventures on board.

- Create a class collage of their journey or of the whole poem.

Resourcing Further Drama from Poetry

Poetry is a rich resource for drama. Frequently condensed, poems focus on issues which can be examined, places which can be visited or people who can be brought to life. Much poetry offers a strong sense of rhythm and beat and lends itself to dramatic presentation, which interprets the words and represents the meanings. There are different ways of using poems for classroom drama, these include:

1 Focus on People, Place or Predicament

Poems can be used for classroom drama when the verses provide a starting point, and suggest places, predicaments or people involved in a situation. Drama investigates human concerns in a fictional context and so the poem acts as a trigger for an unfolding drama, as in 'Through That Door'. We recommend:

'Monster Crazy' by Brian Moses (1998) in *Performance Poems,* Southgate.

'Alone in the Grange' by Gregory Harrison in *Exploring Poetry 5 - 8,* Jan Ballam and Brian Merrick (1991), NATE.

The Train Ride by June Crebbin (1995) illustrated Stephen Lambert, Southgate, Walker.

'On Some Other Planet' by John Rice and 'The Land of Nod' by Robert Louis Stevenson in *First Poems* compiled by Julia Eccleshare (1998) Orchard.

'I Din Do Nuttin' by John Agard and 'Micky Always', in *I Din Do Nuttin and Other Poems,* by John Agard (1983) illustrated by S. Gretz, Magnet.

2 Focus on Narrative Verse

Narrative verse can be used as a guide to provide a complete structure for the drama, or just the title or the first few verses can be read and an improvisational drama planned from this. The poem itself can be read in full afterwards. We recommend:

The Hairy Toe, Anon, illustrated by Daniel Postgate (1998) Walker.

'The Beast from Below' by Allan Ahlberg (1988) in *The Mighty Slide,* Viking, Kestrel.

The Monster Bed by Jeanne Willis (1986) illustrated by Susan Varley, Beaver Books.

'Jim, Who Ran Away From His Nurse, and Was Eaten by a Lion' by Hilaire Belloc and 'The Jumblies' by Edward Lear in *First Poems,* compiled by Julia Eccleshare (1996) Orchard Books.

'The Rescue', by Ian Serraillier in *A First Poetry Book* compiled by John Foster (1979) Oxford University Press.

The Pied Piper of Hamelin by Robert Browning, illustrated by Andre Amstutz (1993) Orchard.

3 Focus on Dance Drama

Poems can be explored with music and action as dance drama. Such work seeks to create a sense of atmosphere and evoke the words in shape, rhythm and percussion, but can also include improvisational work. Examples include:

'Sea Timeless Song' by Grace Nichols (1988) in *Come into My Tropical Garden,* A & C Black.

All Join In by Quentin Blake (1990) Red Fox.

Chapter 4

A PICTURE BOOK: HOW THE BIRDS CHANGED THEIR FEATHERS, BY JOANNA TROUGHTON

Introduction

This drama is based upon a traditional tale of the Arawak people of South America, which has been written up and turned into a beautiful picture book by Joanna Troughton. The myth explains how the birds, originally all white, gained their many colours. It is an allegory, which portrays human wilfulness and draws upon notions of both courage and cowardice, through exploring the consequences of man's broken promise to honour the natural world of the birds.

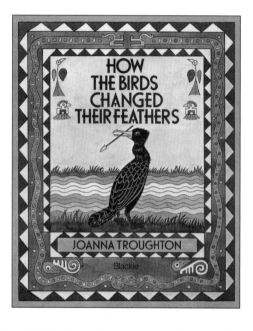

The story tells how a boy, disregarding his mother's warning, continues to hunt birds and receives a dreadful 'come–uppance'. One day, whilst hunting near the river, he finds a pile of coloured beads and threads them onto a string, which he places around his neck. This transforms him into a deadly rainbow snake. The snake preys upon all living things, and the people and animals of the forest live in fear of it. The only creature prepared to fight the snake is a cormorant, who makes a pact with the chief of the human tribe, that if it is successful in killing the snake, then its reward will be the possession of the snake's rainbow skin. The cormorant kills the snake, but is mocked by the chief who breaks his promise to give the bird the skin, laughing at the bird whom he knows cannot carry the long snake skin away. However, the cormorant calls up all the other birds to help, and they swoop down carrying the skin into the sky, to the infuriation of the humans. The myth explains that as they flew, their white feathers took on the colourful hues of the rainbow snake and they became the many different coloured species on the earth today.

The drama convention highlighted in this chapter is **role play in pairs**, which involves the children in working together as if they were particular characters in the story. **Teacher in role** is also used in order to maintain a dramatic direction and pace. The story is read in parts and at appropriate moments, drama is developed to fill the gaps of meaning, to enrich their understanding of the tale by creating the language of the unsaid.

Avoiding the children's suggestions and responses in order to follow the plan may mean that real opportunities for relevant learning are missed. A professional balance between teaching objectives and children's interests is always required.

Teaching Objectives and Learning Areas

- Comment upon each others' drama (*reflection*)
- Become familiar with role play in pairs (*the drama processes*)
- Use language to retell events in role (*language*).

Prior Experience and Materials

- A class science focus on birds or animals, and experience of other myths explaining how various animals gained their stripes, shells or tails would support this drama, but are not essential.
- A copy of the book *How The Birds Changed Their Feathers* by Joanna Troughton (1976), Blackie… . The children should not know the story
- Photocopies of one double page spread from the text: pages 21-22.

First Encounters: Creating the Drama Context

THE BOY GOES HUNTING

- Remind the children of their work on birds, or discuss with them birds they know and their colours. Identify South America on a map/globe.
- Show them the picture book, explain the story's Guyanan origin and that it will be the basis for their drama and story making.
- Read the opening page and show the double page spread which illustrates the birds without their coloured plumage.
- Ask the children to find a partner and role play the conversation the mother has with her son, as she enquires why he is going into the forest with his bow and arrow. What might she say to dissuade him?
- As a class, ask everyone to creep around miming the hunting of the birds in the forest.
- Suggest that one child creeps through the forest in role as the boy, while the rest of the class find a space to stay very still in, as the birds frozen in fright in the trees. Go up to a few children and ask them to voice the birds' thoughts and birds' feelings as the boy creeps nearer them.

Conflicts and Tensions: Developing the Drama

THE DREADED RAINBOW SERPENT

- Read and show the second double page spread in which the wicked boy finds the beautiful multicoloured beads and threads them onto a long grass reed.
- Ask the children to mime this, and as they do so, walk amongst them enquiring about the colours of the beads they are threading, are there any precious or semi-precious stones amongst them?
- Read or narrate the boy's transformation into the rainbow snake and encourage the children to similarly transform themselves as you speak, and to finally slither into the river.
- Ask the children in small groups to make statues of the terrible rainbow snake as it pounces upon some unsuspecting prey.
- Follow this up by reading the next two double pages in the book and show them the illustrations, up to and including the opening sentence of the next page, when the Chief of the Indians calls the animals together.

THE CHIEF APPEALS TO THE ANIMALS

- In role as Chief of the Indians, hold a meeting with the animals of the jungle. Speak to the children as if they were the animals gathering to find out what has happened and ask them what can be done to rid the forest of this menacing creature. In role, try to prompt the children to tell you what they know about the snake, have any of them seen him, how quick was he, what do they want to do, why do they think the boy was turned into a snake? Discuss all this within the context of the whole class improvisation. When you close the meeting, promise solemnly as the Chief that you will give the beautiful rainbow snake skin to whomsoever rids the village of this frightful serpent.

- Read or narrate that the animals made various excuses to avoid trying to kill the snake. Out of role, discuss the excuses the children use at home to avoid doing what they are asked to do by their parents, and ask them to invent some of the animals' excuses.

- Ask everyone to choose an animal who attended the meeting and make a statue of it, and as you circulate around in role as the Chief ask for their help. As they offer their excuse engage in some dialogue with them as appropriate. Only ask around a third of the class, so that the overall pace of the drama is maintained.

- Read to them the excuses made by the animals in the book, and discuss whether they think the snake was eventually defeated and if so how did it happen? Discuss their ideas and remind them of the story setting, so they suggest realistic solutions within the context of the story.

- Ask the children, in small groups' to improvise or create a freeze frame of their solution. Ask each group to explain their plans briefly and reflect upon each other's ideas.

- Choose whether you wish to use their predictions and suggestions, or return to Joanna Troughton's retelling. If the former, build the drama around the issues the children are interested in, and help them solve how the birds changed their feathers. If the latter, tell them that in Joanna's retelling only the cormorant, a diving bird, was prepared to risk his life in order to kill the rainbow snake. He risked his life and believed the Chief would give him the skin, if he succeeded.

THE CHIEF BREAKS HIS PROMISE

- Read or tell this section of the tale in which the cormorant dives deep down, kills the serpent and swims to the riverside with the body. Then the courageous bird goes to the Chief to claim his reward.

- In role as the Chief, make clear your treacherous nature and disdainful attitude. Of course the cormorant can have the skin, if he can carry it away! You will give it instead to the young people for head-dresses and beautiful bangles. In any case what would a little bird like him want with such a skin! Be brief about this, but it will serve as useful preparation for their role play.

- Pair the children up and give each pair a copy of the double page spread showing the bird and the Chief, this will help them generate ideas for a role play.

- In these pairs, role-play the Chief's conversation with the cormorant, showing how he makes excuses in order to trick the bird out of his reward, and encourage elaboration by the children. Listen to a few snippets and extracts of these, and encourage the children to comment on each other's words and ideas.

Resolutions: Drawing the Drama Together

THE CLEVER BIRDS

- Gather the children together and discuss their suggestions about how this small bird could possibly carry away the huge snakeskin.

- Read the story to the end, revealing how the birds got their coloured feathers and discuss the colours of tropical birds such as parrots, macaws, toucans and birds of more temperate climates.

- In pairs, role-play the Chief telling the boy's mother about the day's events. Within the story her situation is not addressed and this could be a means of supporting her in the loss of her son. Some preliminary consideration and preparation within the class may help this.

- Conclude by considering the importance of promises, and the nature of good faith as it is shown in this tale. Share parallels in other stories, and encourage the children to make connections with their own lives, and share these with partners and/or the class.

Extension Activities

- In pairs, ask the children to record on tape one of the role-plays from the drama eg. the mother talking to her son, the cormorant and the Chief, the mother and the Chief.

- Draw pictures of the boy hunting whilst his mother watches. Add speech or thought bubbles.

- Explore other myths from around the world by Joanna Troughton, in literacy time or in drama, e.g. *How Rabbit Stole the Fire* or *How Night Came*, both published by Blackie.

- Develop art and craftwork related to colour, camouflage and display, using the rainbow serpent and the birds.

Resourcing Further Drama from Picture Books

Picture books are a rich source base for dramatic investigation as they tend to be short stories some of which contain one major predicament. Below are some picture books and some suggestions for using them, although they could be used in different ways.

1   Taking the Book as a Guide

Read the story and share the pictures, stopping intermittently to allow the children to find out more about the characters, the conflict or the issues in the story. After some dramatic exploration the next part of the story is read, and then investigated through drama. The tale works to guide the drama, but re-enactment is not sought, instead the children journey alongside the tale, improvise the gaps and flesh out the meanings.

Bob Graham (1992) *Rose Meets Mr Wintergarten*, Walker

Rose Summers and her family move in next door to old Mr Wintergarten's dark mansion. She hears stories about him and then loses her ball in his garden. Will he make friends? A selfish giant type tale, well written, with evocative illustrations. Useful for exploring truth and rumours, loneliness and friendship.

Jeanne Willis (1986) *The Monster Bed*, illustrated by Susan Varley, Beaver

Dennis the monster is scared of the dark and terrified of humans, nothing his mum does seems to comfort him. The class, in role as doctors can enter the text to offer advice about how Dennis can get to sleep at night and what will rid him of this fear. The story, written in narrative verse ends when a young boy, truanting from school, ventures into the cave and meets Dennis. The fear his family feel in his absence, and the consequent hunt for him are also worth exploring.

Michael Foreman (1994) *Jack's Fantastic Voyage*, Red Fox

Jack's grandfather is a sea captain who tells tales of his adventures on the high seas. One night it seems as if the house sails away and they tour the world together. Their expedition can be explored more fully through drama.

2 Creating Their Own Tale from the Opening Scenario

Read or tell the first part of a tale and then move into drama mode and explore the unfolding events, the predicaments and perspectives of all involved. The author's tale can be read at a later date, when the class have finished co-authoring their own tale.

Martin Waddell (1990) *The Hidden House*, Walker

An old man makes three wooden dolls for company, they sit on the window ledge and watch him garden. Early in the text he leaves and doesn't return, the house becomes overgrown and hidden, but how do the dolls cope alone, whom might they meet?

Anthony Browne (1976) *Through the Magic Mirror*, Macmillan

Toby, bored and lonely, walks through a magic mirror in his house into an alternative world where the laws of nature do not apply. Using the same initial device, the class can enter the world of the book and create their own adventures, returning safely home afterwards.

Dennis Reader (1989) *A Lovely Bunch of Coconuts*, Walker

On a small island lives a man in the shade of a coconut tree. On the mainland, a greedy king desires the island and the coconuts — he plots to take over. Good for creating their own tales of his attempts, does he succeed? They can compare their version with the author's ideas.

3 Creating a Follow Up Tale

Read the complete tale and then create a drama which is built on the shoulders of the tale by extending aspects of it. The themes in the original text can be revisited through the follow up and be examined and experienced in action.

John Burningham (1977) *Come Away from the Water Shirley*, Red Fox

Shirley adventures on the high seas whilst her parents doze on the beach. But where did she go on the next day of her holiday? Did she visit a castle, a water park, a funfair, the caves? Endless potential and good for exploring responsibility.

Dieter Schubert (1988) *Where is Monkey?* Beaver

A wordless picture book in which a young boy's beloved cloth monkey is lost and finally found. In the meantime he experiences a number of adventures when rats, hedgehogs and a magpie treat him as their plaything. Excellent for exploring the further adventures of monkey and examining loss, uncertainty, fear and relief.

Jez Alborough (1999) *My Friend Bear*, Walker

In this, the third adventure of Eddy, his teddy and the great big bear, we learn about their developing friendship and some of the games they play together. This is an excellent opportunity to create the next tale of their adventures. Might Eddy meet the bear's family or vice versa? What problems would be encountered if the bear came to Eddy's birthday party?

Chapter 5

A TRADITIONAL TALE: BIMWILI AND THE ZIMWI

Joshua Bimwili and the Zimwee.

1 Bimwili gos to the oston
once upon a time bimwili,
went to the sea her sister
swam in the sea Bimwili
didn't. A big wave washed a
sheel Neer hor feet. She picked
it up and looked inside it
WAs pink.

2 Bimwili looses her sheol
An hour later, The two
sisters ran up thay Grabed
her and ran off. Bimwili
remembed her shell.
She pulled he sisters
bace.

Bimwili gets cout and escapes.
Bimwili got coat by the Zimwee and put in a box
and tock her to the vileid (he didn't No that he went to
her vilig) ra-a-ta-ra her sisters heard her sing
and saved her. THe ENd

Joshua (aged 6)

Bimwili and the Zimwee

Once upon a time there lived a girl called
Bimwili. She had two sister called Tete and Tashi, and a mother
and father.
One day Tete and Tashi came busting in throug the open
door, into the room were there mother was working.
Can we go down to the ocean they said.
Only if you take Bimwili with you said there mother.
They had a bit of a agument.
In the end Tete and Tashi agred to take Bimwili.
So they went to the ocean.
Wile her sisters swum in the ocean, she sitt on a log.
A big wave gave her a shell.
She sang a song about her shell
Her sister's came running up the beach
and grapped one of her arms.
She pulled them back and went back to
get her shell.
By the time Tete and Tashi got back
to the vilig, Bimwili was traped by the
Zimwee.

Tom (aged 7)

Introduction

This drama uses as its source a traditional Swahili tale. The retelling explores relationships and individuality and offers the children the chance to empathise and express in their own words their thoughts and insights about the main character. There is a retelling of the tale at the end of this chapter.

The tale focuses on Bimwili, a physically challenged youngster, who has a positive outlook despite her difficulties. One day, Bimwili and her sisters go down the jungle path to the ocean, they enjoy the sand and the sea and Bimwili finds a beautiful conch shell on the beach, which it seems has been left especially for her. In the twilight hour on their return to the village, Bimwili realises she has left her shell behind and eventually decides to go back to collect it. There she encounters the strange Zimwi, who imprisons her in his drum and commands her to sing to earn him money. Eventually, Bimwili is saved from the Zimwi and is reunited with her family.

The drama conventions of **teacher as storyteller** and **decision alley** are highlighted here as these help to explore the emotions and perspectives of the characters. In the former, the teacher helps shape the drama, provides narrative connections and reflects upon various characters' views. In the latter, one character's inner feelings and conflicts are voiced by the class in an attempt to reflect the complexity of decision making at a particular point in the tale.

This drama is made up of predominantly female roles and you may be concerned that the boys in your class will feel a little alienated from the situation. Our experience with children of this age is that they have no problem with cross-gender role play. If you think that this might be a difficulty then narrate the same story with a brother and a sister. The story is used to guide the drama and is told in sections, so that the gaps and possibilities in the text can be identified and constructed through the drama. Throughout, the story structure frames and leads the children's dramatic investigation, this provides considerable support for the teacher and the class.

Avoiding the children's suggestions and responses in order to follow the plan may mean that real opportunities for relevant learning are missed. A professional balance between teaching objectives and children's interests is always required.

Teaching Objectives and Learning Areas
- Develop empathy and understanding of the main character (*personal and social skills*)
- Recall significant moments in the drama (*reflection*)
- Participate in a decision alley (*the drama processes*).

Prior Experience and Materials
- The children should *not* know the story
- An enlarged copy of Bimwili's two songs
- A large sea shell.

First Encounters: Creating the Drama Context
PLAYING IN THE VILLAGE
- As storyteller, begin the tale, sharing the essence of the first paragraph.
- Ask the children, in groups of three, to show a freeze frame of Bimwili and her two sisters Tasha and Teté at play. In commenting upon these, highlight the contrast between the physically active sisters and the more sedentary and solitary role Bimwili is obliged to take.
- Retell the second paragraph and briefly discuss why Bimwili's mother insisted that Bimwili should accompany her sisters on their trip to the sea.
- Explain to the class you are going into role as one of the sisters, to try and persuade your mother, who will be the class, to let you go without Bimwili. They will have rehearsed mum's arguments in the previous discussion so you should be able to challenge them and help extend their ideas.
- Take up the telling of the tale and use their ideas, eg. *The girls tried their best to persuade their mother, but she had said that…*
- In role as the sisters, let the children in their qroups of three, discuss what they might do in the jungle and at the sea.
- Conclude these improvised conversations by continuing the narrative and describe the girls entering the jungle.

THROUGH THE JUNGLE TO THE OCEAN
- Continue the tale and invite the children to participate in the storytelling by suggesting animals which the sisters heard… Could it have been a lion or a bear growling, was that a toucan or a macaw, high above them in the canopy?
- In small groups, let the class make noises that might be heard in the jungle. Provide time to prepare and then orchestrate these into the narration, creating an atmosphere of uncertainty and tension along the jungle path.

- As storyteller, move the tale onwards to the beach, where Bimwili finds her shell, plays with it and dances around it on the sand. As a class, sing the song together (from an enlarged copy), circle around a real shell on the floor of the classroom.

- Tell more of the tale and prompt the children to mime the actions you're describing: sprinkling the shell with sand, listening to the sea whispering in the shell and daydreaming in the hot sunshine.

- Freeze the children as Bimwili holding her shell, wishing and hoping. Walk around and tell the children that when you touch them you'd like them to share Bimwili's thoughts, desires and daydreams.

Conflicts and Tensions: Developing the Drama

BIMWILI'S TEMPTATION

- As storyteller, relate how as dusk begins to fall Tasha and Teté rush up the beach and hurry her into the jungle to hasten home. Include within your description a vague sense of threat, such as the shadows which seemed to make strange shapes. This atmosphere will spread to the relationship between the sisters. When Bimwili remembers her shell and wants to return for it, her sisters refuse to accompany her. She has to decide what to do.

- Create a decision alley to explore Bimwili's position. Ask the children to form two lines facing each other to make the path in the jungle and use their hands as vines. Ask for a volunteer to be Bimwili. This child will walk slowly along the jungle path made by the other children, and hear her thoughts and fears spoken out loud by the vines as she seeks to make a decision. Give the children time to think of something to say and tell someone next to them. Make suggestions yourself too: *Will mum be cross? Will the shell still be there? Should I run back and join my sisters? I'm scared. What's that noise?* The children might need some ideas to prompt them and then will find their own thoughts and concerns through discussion with each other. Preparation time is essential.

- Undertake the decision alley slowly and deliberately, with the children voicing Bimwili's thoughts as the child in role as Bimwili walks by. Then ask Bimwili what is her decision, to go back for her beautiful shell or go home with her sisters?

- If Bimwili says she'd go on to collect her shell, then continue the drama as described. If Bimwili says she'd go back to join her sisters you have two options. Either accept the decision and leave the tale behind, letting the children take control of the direction of their drama, with you exploring points of dramatic significance as they arise. Or you could narrate that her desperate attempt to join her sisters failed because they had run on too far, and a strange whistling sound tempted her back towards the ocean and her precious shell. Then continue to let the tale guide the drama.

- Ask the children to show what might happen to Bimwili in small group freeze frames. Share these with each other.

THE DANGEROUS STRANGER

- As storyteller, weave in their ideas about Bimwili's possible predicament and then introduce her encounter with the dangerous stranger, the Zimwi.

- In role as the Zimwi, try to be persuasive and wheedling rather than threatening or greedy. Treat the class as Bimwili and ask her to sing to you, for you have heard her lovely song.

- Thank Bimwili in role, and as storyteller explain how the Zimwi captures poor Bimwili. Ask the class to imagine how Bimwili felt, trapped inside the dark drum with only her precious shell for company. Suggest everyone huddles up small, and thinks about how it would feel to be imprisoned in a hot and uncomfortable drum, only allowed out at night in the darkness of the jungle. Slowly count down from 5 to 1 and ask all the children to think out loud very quietly as if they were Bimwili. No one will hear anyone else, but these oral monologues will help the children articulate Bimwili's thoughts and fears. Join in yourself.

- Ask the children how Bimwili feels and discuss her emotions.

Resolutions: Drawing the Drama Together

A MISSING SISTER

- Suggest the children role-play (in threes), the conversation between the mother and Tasha and Teté when they return without Bimwili. Alternatively, this could be undertaken as a whole class with teacher in role as the mother and the class as the two girls. As mother, in your initial belief that Bimwili will be a few minutes behind them, avoid excessive anger, but ask why they didn't stick together, how they got separated and as the time goes on become alarmed and begin to plan what action to take.

- Discuss with the class what her family might do when Bimwili fails to return – write up the class's list of suggestions.

- Produce posters that might be taken to the villages nearby or follow another of their suggestions. This could be undertaken individually or in pairs.

Molly (aged 7)

SAFE AT LAST

- As storyteller, complete the tale with the class joining in the Zimwi's rat-a-tat-tats upon his drum and the new song (same tune) which Bimwili sings so mournfully.

- In final freeze frames, ask the groups of three to show Bimwili and her sisters together at the end of the tale. Move around the class and ask a few children to think out loud: what is Bimwili thinking as she makes necklaces with her sisters? How do Tasha and Teté feel now?

- Ask the children to identify significant moments in their drama. What lessons might be learnt from these events? Discuss the connections and parallels which can be found in their lives.

Extension Activities

- Pairs could retell one particularly memorable section of the tale.
- Extracts of the story could be used for further literacy work on a character's behaviour, appearance, words or emotions.
- Create a class emotions map which shows how Bimwili felt during major events in the tale, or a timeline of her changing emotions.
- Storyboards or storymaps could be produced to reflect the story structure.
- The picture book version, retold by Verna Aardema (1985, Macmillan) could be read and compared to your class's version. Susan Meddaugh's illustrations could be used to create thought bubbles for various characters at particular points.
- In art, a 3D Zimwi could be created or various shells examined and drawn.

Thomas (aged 6)

Resourcing Further Drama from Traditional Tales

Traditional tales, told orally, offer a plethora of starting points for drama, and with their strong structures, often polarised characters and clear exploration of themes, they represent rich resource material for drama. In classroom drama it is important that tales which are *not known* by the class are used to avoid direct re-enactment. In oral storytelling there is greater freedom for the teller to weave the children's own ideas and insights created in drama into the unfolding tale.

1 Using an Oral Story to Guide the Drama

The teacher tells the tale, stopping intermittently to find out more about the mood, the conflict or the characters in the story. After some dramatic exploration, the oral story is taken up again by the teacher who incorporates the new knowledge into the retelling and takes the story forward. In this way the tale guides and promotes the drama.

Obi Onyefulu (1997) *Chinye: A West African Folk Tale*, Frances Lincoln
This Nigerian folktale tells of young Chinye, who is forced by her unkind stepsister out into the dark night to collect water. The forest spirits protect her, but are not quite as generous to her spoilt stepsister who disobeys their instructions. This story can be used in several ways, but it offers a particularly strong guide for classroom drama.

Mary Medlicott (1996) The Very Mean King, in *The Big Wide Mouthed Toad-Frog and Other Stories*, Kingfisher
This Kenyan tale uses repetitive story language and actions which encourage joining in. It tells of a mean and sour faced king who wields his authority without a care for the consequences. His come-uppance involves the Rattle of Punishment hidden behind the clouds and the king taking some of his own medicine.

Helen East (1989) *The Singing Sack*, A & C Black
This collection of 28 song-stories from around the world offers a considerable resource for drama. The Andalucian story of The Singing Sack itself is a parallel tale to Bimwili and the Zimwi and suits retelling with frequent stops to explore the tale through drama.

2 Building from a Retold Fragment

The teacher selects an extract from a story to share and the class examine this through classroom drama, investigating the consequences, prior events and issues which surround it. The opening or closing sections can be used or one episode from within the tale. The story provides a dramatic context, but the drama itself shapes their own story which they co-author together.

Pete Seeger (1994) *Abiyoyo*, Simon and Schuster

This is adapted from a South African folktale and involves a boy and his father who like to play, to make magic and music. The dull townsfolk ostracise the family and send them to live on the edge of the village. Later, the great giant Abiyoyo arrives to terrorise the villagers, who are rescued by the little boy (whose music makes the giant dance) and his father (whose magic 'zoop' stick makes him disappear). Re-telling an early extract from this tale enables the class to explore issues around 'difficult' neighbours.

Anne Grifalconi (1986) *The Village of Round and Square Houses*, Picture Mac

This picture book explains the story behind the real village of Tos in Cameroon, West Africa, where the men live in square houses and the women in round. The existence of this village can be explained and some pictures shown so that the class can create the story behind this separation of the sexes. The tale in the text can later be shared.

Tony Fairman (1991) 'The Man with a Tree on his Head' in *Bury My Bones But Keep My Words*, Collins

An amusing tale from Botswana about a selfish man who lets his wife do all the work. One morning he awakes to find a mopane tree growing on his head, which will not go away until he mends his ways. Try retelling the opening section and explore his laziness.

Liz Weir (1995) 'Wee Meg Barnileg' in *Boom Chic a Boom: A Book of Stories and Rhymes to Share*, O'Brien (Also available on tape and CD)

This Irish retelling recounts how Wee Meg Barnileg, a spoilt only child, behaves so badly, is so rude and unkind to animals that finally the fairy folk decide to capture her and teach her a few manners. In the world of the fairies, she learns much before returning to her parents. Building from a fragment when the fairies capture her, the theme in the tale can be explored in flashbacks, flashforwards, improvisations and dramatic explorations.

3   **Telling the Whole Tale then Exploring the Language of the Unsaid**

The tale is told, then selected parts of it are revisited through drama. So the gaps in the text such as leaps in the narrative, which cross undeveloped weeks or months, or characters' unrecorded conversations are created retrospectively. Working on these elements can deepen the children's understanding and illuminate the meanings. In Bimwili and the Zimwi for example, what happened during those seven weeks when the little girl travelled with the Zimwi?

Paul Owen Lewis (1995) *Storm Boy*, Barefoot Books

This picture book tells the story of an Indian prince who falls out of a canoe during a thunderstorm off the Pacific Coast of North America. The hero's adventures beneath the waters explore the lack of distinction between animals and humans and the rites of passage. The powerful visuals support the tale and could be used to help the children explore the unwritten text and enrich their understanding.

Mary Medlicott (1996) *The King With Dirty Feet and other Stories*, Kingfisher

The title story in this book is a clever retelling of a tale about a king who hates getting his feet dirty. His ministers one by one suggest strategies to avoid this, but each fail until one invents the shoe. A clearly structured tale which can be told and retrospectively revisited.

Andrew Fusek Peters (1997) *Strange and Spooky Stories*, Barefoot Books
The nine surreal and spooky stories in this book include one from the Czech Republic called Otesahnek the Wooden Doll, who comes to life and is very hungry. She is so hungry she eats more than her fair share. Eventually however, she receives her just deserts and her victims are saved. A strong tale to tell, revisit and explore.

A TRADITIONAL TALE: BIMWILI AND THE ZIMWI

It wasn't in your time, it wasn't in my time, but it was in somebody's time that there lived a little girl called Bimwili. Bimwili was the youngest in her family and was mostly full of songs and laughter, although sometimes she'd watch her two sisters Tasha and Teté a-hopping, a-skipping and a-jumping and wish that she could be like them. For you see Bimwili had a quirky leg, a leg that didn't work quite properly, a leg she had to drag behind her as she walked. So she couldn't join in with her sisters' dancing and prancing, even though she wanted to very much indeed. Instead, Bimwili learnt to thread exquisite necklaces out of melon and papaya seeds, to weave fabulous stories and to cook delicious meals with sweet smelling spices.

One day Tasha and Teté tried to persuade their mother to allow them to go down to the ocean together to swim.
'We'll stay on the jungle path.'
'We'll be back before night fall.'
'We'll swim together at all times.'
'Oh mother, please let us go, just us two.'

But their mother would not give her permission unless they took young Bimwili with them as well. Her sisters objected and told their mother that Bimwili would slow them down, that she would hold them back and that she couldn't swim anyway. But their mother held firm, insisting they were not allowed to go unless Bimwili accompanied them. So, sometime later, the three sisters set off together. Their mother gave them slices of paw paw for the journey. 'Remember', she admonished them, 'don't stray off the jungle path, keep together at all times, and start back well before dusk begins to fall. I'll be looking out for you.'

The path through the jungle was clearly marked at first, but after a while, thick leaf fronds and vines twined across the jungle floor and poor Bimwili had to be helped over these. From high in the treetops above them the girls heard strange sounds, and once they thought they saw the stripey skin of a boa constrictor camouflaged in the undergrowth.

When the path finally opened out, the shimmering sea and white sands spread before them. Bimwili had never been down to the ocean before. She was enchanted. Whilst Tasha and Teté rushed to the water's edge and plunged headlong into the frothing mouth of the ocean, Bimwili found a log to sit on and let her fingers and toes explore the warm grains of sand.

Wave after wave crashed down upon the sand, and the salt spray sprinkled her face with tiny freckles of moisture as she listened to the pounding of the sea on the shore. Once, when a crescent shaped wave crashed onto the beach and its water was sucked back into the sea, there in front of her, she found a beautiful pink conch shell, the like of which she had never seen before. Delighted, she picked it up and ran her fingers over its smooth inner surface, then, holding it to her ear, she heard the mysterious murmuring and far off gossip of the sea. Placing the shell carefully back on the sand, Bimwili circled it, singing:

> *'I have a shell from out of the sea,*
> *A shell the big wave gave to me,*
> *It's pink inside like the sunset sky,*
> *And if you listen, you'll hear the ocean sigh.'*

Bimwili was so pleased with her new possession, she hugged it to her chest and scooped up sand, scattering it into the shell and making faint patterns and rhythms on its smooth and irridescent surface. Setting it gently on the sand, she again rested on the log and began to dream, to wonder and imagine in the hot sunshine.

Time passed, as time is wont to do, and when the sun began to make its slow descent in the sky, the two older sisters suddenly realised they must make a hasty return. They rushed up the beach, collected Bimwili and hurried her back onto the jungle path. It was only when the three girls paused for a moment's rest, that Bimwili realised she had left her shell on the sand. She begged Tasha and Teté to return with her, but they absolutely refused to do so and told her to fetch it herself if she must, for they wanted to get back to the village before twilight.

Poor Bimwili, she didn't know what to do, she was afraid to walk the jungle path alone in the dusk, but in her mind's eye she could see her shell gleaming and beckoning her, so she limped back the way she had come, singing her song to reassure herself.

> *'I have a shell from out of the sea,*
> *A shell the big wave gave to me,*
> *It's pink inside like the sunset sky,*
> *And if you listen, you'll hear the ocean sigh.'*

However, back on the beach, sitting silhouetted on her log, was the strangest creature you could ever imagine. It was the Zimwi. The Zimwi was tall, thin and upright with dark popping eyes and strange long arms covered in tree bark, out of which stretched fine twig-like fingers.

'Aaah, Bimwili,' he exclaimed with satisfaction, 'I have been waiting for you, I'm glad you returned my dear...'

'I came back for my sh..sh.. shell sir, my beautiful shell, sir,' stuttered Bimwili in reply. She could not see it anywhere, yet she had surely left it here beside the log.

'Aaah yes, the shell,' gloated the Zimwi, his eyes alight with glee, 'I took the liberty of placing that in my drum here, for safe keeping. Look!'

Bimwili stepped forward cautiously and peered inside the open drum. A faint pink glow shone in the dark depths of the drum.

'Perhaps you would sing for me, my own little one?' invited the Zimwi somewhat threateningly and so Bimwili, assuming this was some kind of bargain, began falteringly to sing.

> *'I have a shell from out of the sea,*
> *A shell the big wave gave to me,*
> *It's pink inside like the sunset sky,*
> *And if you listen, you'll hear the ocean sigh.'*

'Such dulcet tones,' noted the Zimwi with a slight nod of his head. But when Bimwili stretched into the drum to retrieve her precious shell, he leant forward and pushed her forcibly down, down, down, deep into the drum's depths. In almost the same moment, he snapped on the lid and secured it fast. Poor Bimwili was trapped inside!

'Now,' exclaimed the Zimwi with satisfaction, 'When I play on my magic singing drum, people will come from all around to hear it sing, to hear *you* sing! Aahah! Aahah! I shall never be hungry again!'

The very next day, he took the drum to a nearby village, stretched out his long twiggy fingers and drummed out 'arat arat ara-ta-ta-tat', calling everyone to come and listen. From deep inside the drum, Bimwili hugged her shell and sang her song again and again. The Zimwi was paid handsomely for sharing his magic singing drum. That night he returned to the jungle, and released Bimwili into another kind of darkness. He fed her fruits and berries, but warned her not to stray for fear of the wild animals.

In the days and weeks that followed, the Zimwi travelled from village to village, drumming out 'arat arat ara-ta-ta-tat' and earning food and money from the people who came to hear his magical singing drum. Each night he returned to the jungle and let Bimwili out. She did not try to escape for she could not run far and she knew not which way to venture in the darkness. Many adventures befell her and the Zimwi as they travelled together, one free, one trapped, but each dependent upon the other.

One day, seven long weeks after her capture, the Zimwi came to Bimwili's village carrying his magic drum. He set it down in the market place and gave her the sign to sing, 'arat arat ara-ta-ta-tat'. So often had he heard the tune, that he did not notice the words had changed, as Bimwili sang soulfully.

'I had a shell from out of the sea,
A shell the Zimwi stole from me,
It's dark inside like the midnight sky,
And if you listen, you'll hear Bimwili cry.'

Bimwili's sisters, skipping in the yard outside, heard the words and stopped in their tracks. They listened once more to their sister's message, then raced to their mother as fast as their feet would carry them. Making her way through the crowd Bimwili's mother heard her missing daughter's mournful lament.

'I had a shell from out of the sea,
A shell the Zimwi stole from me,
It's dark inside like the midnight sky,
And if you listen, you'll hear Bimwili cry.'

'Why Mr Zimwi sir,' said Bimwili's mother, a faint smile spreading across her face. 'Your drum is magical indeed! What do you prefer sir, fish or fowl?'

'Why some fish thank you, lightly broiled fish would be very pleasant,' he replied.

The Zimwi accompanied Bimwili's mother to choose his fish and while they were gone, Tasha and Teté worked together to unclasp the drum, and help their delighted sister out. They hid her safely in the bushes, then placing three large stones inside the drum, refitted the lid and awaited the Zimwi's return.

Having enjoyed a good meal, the Zimwi thought he would treat the people of the village to another song from his drum, so he raised his twig-like fingers, 'arat arat ara-ta-ta-tat!' No sound came from within. 'Arat arat ara-ta-ta-tat' he drummed urgently upon the lid. People began to laugh, had his drum lost its magic powers they asked? Was it merely a trick? 'Arat arat ara-ta-ta-tat' he tried again, but all in vain. Utterly humiliated, the Zimwi took the drum back to the jungle, shouting all the while at Bimwili whom he believed was still inside. When he opened it and found it was *he* who had been tricked, he was even more furious and vowed never to deal with humans again.

Meanwhile, Bimwili and her two sisters, her family and indeed the whole community were celebrating her safe return. The precious pink shell was filled with mango juice and passed around for all to drink. There was much singing and storytelling, much clapping and cheering, much laughter and loving, now that young Bimwili was home at last.

Tasha and Teté never quite forgot that time, for in her absence, they found they had missed Bimwili's company, her stories and her songs, her generous nature and her pleasure in living. They made friends anew with their forgiving sister and found time to play her games, to listen to her stories, and to sing with her. They were happy just to be together.

Chapter 6

A HISTORICAL THEME: THE KING WHO WAS AFRAID

Introduction

This drama focuses upon castles and their role and function in history. It explores their physical features, why they were necessary and examines the life of those who lived in them. In particular, the relationship between a king and his daughter is investigated. Charles Keeping's illustrations of Tennyson's *The Lady of Shalott* (1986, Oxford University Press) are used as an additional resource in the drama.

The drama, which could be undertaken over two sessions, begins with the king, expressing his anxiety about the bands of robbers who have been roaming the countryside, stealing and trouble making. This monologue sets the scene and prompts the children to offer advice and create solutions. Having created a secure fortress, the children inhabit the castle and encounter challenges within it. In the second session, when the drama opens out they are given one of Keeping's illustrations from the text which shows a strange light shining from the castle. In role as travellers, they investigate this and find a girl, alone and unhappy, shown through another of his sensitive illustrations. Through talking to her and her father, the king, the children investigate her role and the expectations of women like her in history.

The drama convention highlighted here is **drawing in role**, as both pictures and diagrams provide additional information about the setting which is collectively created. **Writing in role** is also used to develop empathy with the princess's plight.

Teaching Objectives and Learning Areas

- Offer ideas to develop the fiction (*the imagination*)
- Use language to question, enquire and empathise (*language*)
- Make connections and comparisons with the past (*reflection*).

Prior Experience and Materials

- The children need some knowledge to draw upon, so the drama would be best undertaken during a history focus on castles. A visit to a real castle would be advantageous
- A simple crown
- Letters, some of which are embossed or crested
- Pencils and paper for lists
- An easel and paper
- The book of *The Lady of Shalott* illustrated by Charles Keeping, Oxford University Press
- Photocopies of pictures from *The Lady of Shalott*.

First Encounters: Creating the Drama Context

ROBBERS ABOUND, WE NEED A SAFE HOUSE

- Begin the drama in role as a queen/king (with a simple crown) holding some letters, and pacing up and down in agitated fashion. You are not conscious of being watched and are talking to yourself about the letters you've received from your people, farmers and noblemen, all of whom have had cows, sheep, jewellery, and money stolen by the gangs of robbers who roam your land. Express serious concerns about lawlessness, how can you protect your people, once you only worried about stolen tarts, but now you have much more to concern you.

- The class will be drawn into the monarch's thinking as they watch. Suddenly notice them and ask them what they're doing, are they spying? Listen to their replies and be seen to be reassured, request that they help you to solve your problem, and seek their advice. List the problems surrounding the big, but ordinary house you live in with its rudimentary security, and suggest you need a stronger, safer house. Could they help design such a house for you, your family and your servants?

- Ask them to make a list or draw sketches of what is needed in pairs. In role as the monarch, visit pairs asking them about their suggestions, and what materials they'd recommend for the building. Enquire where the armour will be kept, how the robbers will be prevented from entering, and how thick the walls will be and so on. This work could be enhanced by support materials and reference books.

- Gather the class together and ask them to bring their lists or drawings to help create a corporate plan. Draw it yourself but be guided by their ideas, discuss the placement of the castle and its general construction, moving gradually to significant details about defence.

- Suggest your advisors tick off their suggestions as they are incorporated into the design. This large diagram will give a common sense of place to the drama and will help you assess their knowledge and identify issues which need clarification.

- Suggest to the children they actually make the castle with their bodies. Make a large circle with the class and ask two children to go into the centre of the empty space and make the shape of some part of the castle you've planned, using their bodies as a kind of sculpture.

- Continue this by asking the rest of the class to join in, gradually building up an image of the castle. Prompt them, if necessary to be expressive with their bodies. Suggest some might like to join together to create parts of the castle, the portcullis or drawbridge for example.

- Circulate fairly rapidly amongst the children, asking them which part of the castle they are and making comments aloud, such as 'What a tall tower this is. It would be hard to climb'. This will encourage uncertain children to join in and share their ideas.

LIVING IN THE CASTLE

- Return to the diagram of the castle and generate further suggestions about the jobs carried out there: blacksmith, falconer, gatekeeper, cooks, maids, friar, bailiff, baker and so on.

- Ask pairs to decide on a job to be undertaken together in the castle and then improvise these jobs and the daily life of the castle. You can join this whole class improvisation in a role, such as a travelling merchant selling goods or as the king surveying his domain. This will sustain the improvisation and allow you to circulate and observe from within the drama.

- Turn your observations into a narration, and include that on this special day something important happened. Ask them to suggest what it was, and let a few ideas be voiced briefly.

- Ask the children in small groups to create a freeze frame of what happened. Altogether, look at each other's freeze frames, noting the main idea behind each.

Tensions and Conflicts: Developing the Drama

THE MYSTERIOUS LIGHT

- Give the children copies of Charles Keeping's illustrations of the castle from Tennyson's *'The Lady of Shalott'*. Ponder over this together and begin to talk about the mood and atmosphere of the castle and what kind of place it is. Who or what might be the cause of the light? Discuss their ideas.

- Suggest to the class that they could be travellers from another country, who have never seen a castle and who come across this one, which they decide to visit in the morning. It is nearly nightfall so they need a meal and a rest. Narrate that the travellers gathered together to eat on the banks of the river and talked well into the dark night about the source of the mysterious light and the huge castle. Use their ideas in your storytelling, and suggest that when they finally slept their dreams were full of possibilities.

- Narrate their waking and ask them to tell each other about their dreams. Describe their short journey to the castle, entering by the drawbridge across the moat.

- In role as the king, welcome them, proudly tell them a little about your castle and inform them they can visit every room in the keep, except one locked room near the battlements. This room is closed to preserve the privacy of your family, be quite clear and stress this one rule. Finish by suggesting everyone meets back in the Great Hall.

- Prompt the class to improvise exploring the castle in the drama space, moving amongst them to find out which rooms they are visiting.

THE DISCOVERY AND AN ANGRY FATHER

- Interrupt their improvisation and narrate that a couple of the travellers found themselves at the locked door. (It is quite probable that some of the children will have already 'found' this room.)

Explain that when they peered through the key-hole, they saw a girl sitting alone, her hands in her lap and head bowed, she looked upset and unhappy. You are describing Charles Keeping's illustration of the princess in that pose.

- Give each child a copy of the picture of the princess, and ask them to write what she is thinking in a large thought bubble.

- When the children have nearly finished writing, enter in role as the angry king, saying something to the effect that someone has disobeyed your orders not to go near the room, as visitors they have been discourteous, you trusted them and they let you down. In future, visitors will not be made welcome. Tell them that your daughter, the princess, is kept in her own room for her own good, she is not allowed out unless she is chaperoned. Ask the visitors who it was, and why they peered through the keyhole? Can they explain their conduct?

This outburst needs to be made carefully so that the children are not intimidated, but through their sympathy for the girl feel able to ask the king for an explanation for keeping her a virtual prisoner. The children may be ready to question the king or may need some time to formulate their questions. If time is needed, leave for an urgent meeting with your chancellor. If not, conduct the whole class improvisation straight away, becoming more composed, but clear about your views about the place of women in society at that time.

Resolutions: Drawing the Drama Together

THE FAMILY'S EXPECTATIONS

- If the children need to gather their thoughts together, give time in class or pair discussion, to generate questions to ask the king.

- Return as the now more composed king, sit down and respond to the class's questions and enquiries. (In effect the king is now on the hot seat.) Try to explain your views that girls need protection as they are 'weaker', and that there is an expected role for them in your society. The princess has added duties and must marry to help your kingdom by making a good alliance through her marriage, with another power. Then she must have a son to secure the succession and so on.

- Conclude the discussion by arguing the princess does not mind her situation, she knows it's her duty. Perhaps they would like to ask her for themselves?

- Invite a child, or another adult to be the princess (or if they can cope with you switching roles, do it yourself), and sit before the travellers in the hot seat. The class will have plenty of questions which you can add to: how

I want to get out of here, I want to run away from him!

Dear God please help me get out. Amen

Jo (aged 6)

42

does she feel, how often is she allowed out, has she friends, does she accept her role or hope for more, what is she looking forward to, does she understand her parents' desire to protect her until they find a suitable husband for her? Does she know if she were a peasant girl she might be freer to make more of her own choices and so on.

- As a class, discuss the issues with reference to the differences between wealthy women and the peasants in the past. Shift the perspective to contemporary times to allow personal connections to be made about the roles of men and women.

Extension Activities

- Create a class list of the advantages and disadvantages of being in the princess's position.
- Compare women's clothing in medieval Britain (rich and poor) with clothing in modern times.
- Create a display of traditional and modern 'princess' tales, read these and discuss the roles authors give to their royal princesses.
- The classic poem *The Lady of Shalott* could be used to develop a further drama around the wandering knight and the young woman's death and burial.

Resourcing Further Drama from History

This drama uses and extends the children's knowledge about buildings in the past and the lives of those who lived in them, but other historical resources also provide excellent starting points for drama. These include:

1 Famous People and Events

Significant incidents in the lives of people such as Florence Nightingale, Grace Darling, Dr Barnardo and Guy Fawkes can be explored. Through visiting the past (in a time machine), the children will become more involved in active problem solving in the historical context. For example, re-creating the hospital Florence ran in Scutari and working as nurses cleaning, organising and tending the sick soldiers may involve dealing with problems of limited resources, writing letters to demand more help and examining the consequences of Florence's illness, as well as preparing for her post war meeting with Queen Victoria.

2 Historical Artefacts

First and second hand evidence can usefully be employed to trigger or enrich a drama. We have variously used facsimiles of old documents, a mangle, an iron, Victorian toys, antique jewellery, a spindle, a carding comb, oil lamps and genuine clothing in drama with 5-8 year olds. A physical artefact can make a significant difference, for example Captain Cook could persuade sailors to join him by reassuring them about his knowledge of the sea and showing them how to use his captain's sextant. The challenges of his historical voyage could then be explored.

3 Historical Buildings

Local and national buildings of historical interest provide a further resource. Churches and cathedrals, mines, abbeys, follies, a canal lockhouse, a dockyard, the Houses of Parliament and so on can be used imaginatively as the sites for drama and investigations into the past. The National Trust run drama days in many of their stately homes, which involve the children in costumed improvisations to explore pertinent historical issues.

THE LADY
OF SHALOTT

ALFRED, LORD TENNYSON
ILLUSTRATED BY
CHARLES KEEPING

OXFORD

4 Historical Fiction

Fiction provides another way into history since many such texts focus on how children behaved and were treated in particular eras. They are therefore easy to open up through classroom drama and the children can identify with the characters. Examples we recommend include:

Allan Ahlberg (1998) *Mockingbird*, illus. Paul Howard, Walker.
Helen Cresswell (1995) *A Game of Catch*, Hodder Headline.
Susan Hill (1993) *Beware, Beware*, illus. Angela Barret, Walker.
Frances Thomas (1994) *Mr Bear and the Bear*, illus. Ruth Brown, Red Fox.
Roderick Hunt (1989) Any of the historical 'magic key stories', Oxford Reading Tree.
James Dunbar (1999) *When I was young; one family remembers 300 years of history*, illus. Martin Remphry, Wonderwise, Franklin Watts.

Chapter 7

A LETTER: THE NEW PARK

Introduction

This drama uses a letter of invitation as a hook to stimulate interest and as a resource which casts the children in the role of estate workers in a new park. Letters provide a useful source for drama as they set a context, provide information about the people involved and can sow seeds of possible tension and conflict. They also offer a degree of authenticity, particularly if they are delivered and properly addressed and stamped.

The session focuses upon designing and building a new park, and the challenges which arise when part of the park is vandalised. Can the destruction be sorted out, who are the culprits and how can they be apprehended? The class take up the role of those who work in public parks, but also become police officers and local residents as they seek to examine the appropriate conduct of visitors. This drama offers the children the chance to speak with authority, based upon their knowledge of local amenities, such as parks and playgrounds.

The drama convention of **hot seating** is used to help the children dig beneath the surface of an individual's actions and explore motive, opinion and perspective. **Whole class improvisation** is also extensively used.

Avoiding the children's suggestions and responses in order to follow the plan may mean that real opportunities for relevant learning are missed. A professional balance between following the teaching objectives and children's interests is always required.

Teaching Objectives and Learning Areas

- Explore moral conduct (*personal and social skills*)
- Contribute ideas from the perspective of different roles (*the imagination*)
- Use different language registers in response to different roles (*language*).

Prior Experience and Materials

- A local study (including public amenities such as the park) could advantageously be undertaken prior to the drama, and/or a trip to the local park. However the drama could be undertaken without such a focus, because of the children's own experience of parks.
- Letters addressed to each member of the class, placed in one envelope
- Easel and large paper with an outline of the park area
- Clipboards, pencils and paper
- Ribbon or crepe paper for the Opening Ceremony
- A letter from the Mayor or Mayoress.

First Encounters: Creating the Drama Context

EXPERTS ARE NEEDED

- Discuss the local park as well as other outdoor leisure facilities they know about, such as local football pitches, the swings, fun parks, gardens in stately homes and so on. Which have they visited? Which is their favourite? What is the purpose of these places?

Hexley Council,
Efficiency Rd,
London.
TAX A11
020 8638 7623
http://www.hexlley.gov.uk

Dear .... ,

I am delighted to hear that you have accepted our invitation to join the Parks Department to help with the planning of a new park facility.

As you know, the new park is an exciting adventure and supported by your local council. We asked you to help us because you have the knowledge, talent and skill in many of the areas needed.

These include:

- Children's outdoor sports area
- Food, drink and cafeteria work
- Gardening and flower displays
- Fishing and boating on the lake
- Ice cream sales.

I expect you also have other talents, which we hope to learn about soon.

Please ensure you are not late for our first planning meeting on ....
This will be held in the Conference Centre at Langdon Rd, The Broadway, Hexley.
I look forward to meeting you then.

Yours sincerely,

Matthew Arnold
Senior Parks Manager.

Directorate of Education and Leisure Services

- During the discussion 'remember' that the class received a large envelope that morning and ask them if they want to open it now? Alternatively, arrange for a colleague to arrive with the envelope for the class.

- Hand out the letters inside the envelope, which are addressed to each child in the class. Let the children read their own. Comment to the class they are honoured to be invited to meet the manager of the new park, their expertise is obviously widely known. Make sure your drama symbol (see chapter 15), is clearly visible so the children realise this is part of a drama.

- Alert the class that you are going into role as the Manager of the Parks Department, suggest they bring their chairs to gather round for the meeting. Then welcome them formally to the planning meeting for the new park, which you hope is going to be very distinctive, a cut above the parks already in town. Explain that their first task is to help you firm up the provisional plans for the park. Be specific in referring to the expertise you know exists amongst the group; some were curators in museums, others were restaurant chefs, some were horticulturists in National Gardens and still others have worked in the leisure industry, designing playground areas and so on.

- At this point come briefly out of role and ask them to decide for themselves what their role and expertise might be. Let them discuss these and check that everyone has an idea.

- In pairs, ask them to introduce themselves to each other in role, and tell their new colleague about their previous work experience and why they believe they have been invited to help design the new park.

- In role as the manager, unveil an outline of the park area (previously drawn on a flip chart) and ask them for specific ideas and recommendations. At present, it is just a grassed area with some established trees, one large lake and a decent single storey building. The park has to provide for the young and old in the community. Listen to their suggestions and add symbols and details to the map, letting the experts guide you about where various features should be placed. Agree a name for the park and when the plan is complete, thank them and close the meeting.

Conflicts and Tensions: Developing the Drama

THE LABOUR BEGINS IN EARNEST

- Identify together the key roles and areas of responsibility associated with the park, e.g. the team in charge of the lake may need to set up a boat house, perhaps purchase canoes and rowing boats, order life jackets, as well as stock the lake with fish and so on.

We need more waterproof paint for the boats.

Nelson

- At this point there is a change of role for the children, when you ask them to become employees in the park and form working teams responsible for different areas. Designate areas of the drama space as parts of the park, and ask the teams to get to work. This will involve improvising the jobs which need to be done to prepare their area for the opening. Visit each area and comment upon their labours, the class could watch snippets of these improvisations.

We've nearly finished planning the food. Can we give free ice creams at the opening? People would like it.

Kim

The roses are still in bud – they're not ready. What can we do to make them bloom?

Hannah

- Announce there is a lunchtime meeting in the conference room next to the cafeteria. Suggest they help themselves to sandwiches and sit with their team. In role as the manager, open this meeting, asking each group for a progress report. Do they have any equipment needs, have they encountered any problems? Defer to their experience and ask the advice of the workforce over problems. Make a note of any requirements you agree to purchase.

The play area is great, but the ground is too rough. Children could hurt themselves you know.

Alisdair

(7 year olds)

- At the close of the meeting read out a letter from the Mayor/ess, expressing delight in accepting their kind invitation to the Grand Opening. Since the Mayor/ess asks if any additional events are being put on for the opening, ask your employees for ideas.
- Suggest everyone returns to work and then quite quickly freeze the action. Narrate the passage of time and describe how over the weeks that followed, the gardening specialists planted annuals, the children's play equipment team installed new resources and so on. Try to reflect the children's ideas shared with you earlier and stress the labour, pride and expertise of all involved as the big day arrived.

DISASTER STRIKES ON THE BIG DAY

- Inform the class that on the day itself the park officials and workers all got up early and packed a bag for the day ahead. Prompt them to mime as you narrate this episode.
- Tell them the manager was there first with the key to the gates, and opened them up just as the other employees arrived. Encourage the workers to gather around you as you open the gates. As you unlock the gate, pause, let silence hold sway, followed by your reaction of surprise and dismay. In role, go forward and describe the mess you see in the park. Ask them what they can see e.g. flowers picked and dying, the grass chewed up by bike tracks, litter everywhere, graffiti sprayed on the new play area. You are flabbergasted and can't believe your eyes.
- Urge your workforce to check their area for further vandalism and report back as soon as possible. This will become a whole class improvisation.
- In role as a local police sergeant, draw them together and listen to their problems. Estimate the damage with them and make notes. Ponder with them on how the vandals got in.
- As teacher, ask the children what might the police sergeant do next? Who might be interviewed? How can the facts about last night's events be established?

WHY WOULD SOMEBODY DO THIS?

- Let them improvise their suggestions in small groups. This is likely to involve children in role as police officers interviewing local residents or searching for clues about the culprits amongst the mess, maybe also interviewing the manager or park employees. Use the clipboards for note taking.

  > Well, where were you last night young man?
  > Chloe

- Listen to a few snippets from these and, using their ideas, suggest to the class that one of the possible suspects was brought to the police station later that day for questioning. Suggest to them that they take up roles as police officers and question the individual. Give them time to prepare questions to ask you as a suspect.

  > Why have you got mud all over your trousers and a ripped T-shirt?
  > Abbie

- You are in the hot seat in role as a suspect. Reply to their questions ambiguously, e.g. you noticed the side gate was open, but you can't remember if you went in. Ask the police what the problem is and show surprise at their replies, why shouldn't people ride their bikes in the park? The lake is for fishing, so what's the problem? When you looked in through the gate you didn't see any notices, saying 'keep off the grass' or 'no fishing'. Retain an 'innocent until proved guilty' attitude, after all there were no signs to regulate what can and cannot be done in the park.

  > Have you always lived around here?
  > Mike

  > Does your mother know you were out last night?
  > Lewis

  > How would you like someone to mess up your garden at home?
  > Dom

  > (7 year olds)

Resolutions: Drawing the Drama Together

THE OPENING GOES AHEAD

- As a whole class, improvise repairing the damage ready for the Grand Opening which has been postponed.

- In role as the manager, discuss with your workforce what needs to be done to ensure this is less likely to happen again – what can they do to prompt good behaviour? List their suggestions.

- Taking up their ideas, develop some of them e.g. the officials might produce codes of conduct or signs which could be displayed in the park to encourage orderly behaviour.

- Create a simple Ceremony for the Opening with the Mayor/ess – prepare the ribbon cutting, a speech or a song and dance. A dedication/opening plaque could also be written.

- In role as the Mayor/ess, (this could be another adult), arrive for the opening, take part in the Ceremony and visit each area talking to the workers and congratulating them on their labours.

- As the class teacher, discuss with the children the kind of damage they have seen in their own environment, and their view of such vandalism.

Extension Activities

- In role as park employees, the children could write a letter to a friend telling them about the new park, the problems they encountered, the vandalism and the eventual opening.

- Produce pamphlets advertising the park, including a map of the area, hours of opening, and facilities available.

- Convert the role play area into the information/first aid centre in the park, where problems such as lost/hurt children, loose dogs, and broken equipment can be solved.

Resourcing Further Drama from Letters

Letters and written pamphlets can be a useful prompt for dramatic exploration. Authenticity is a key factor in creating these artefacts and it is worth the time tailoring the resource to the issue and the class and ensuring the letter is 'delivered' appropriately. Letters can also be found *during* classroom drama to provide further information about a character (e.g. a letter might be found in Humpty Dumpty's rucksack), or can be *written from within* a drama (e.g. postcards or letters sent from a seaside holiday). The suggestions below, however, focus on using letters to initiate drama. Such letters can be shaped to suit cross curricular work.

1   Letters/Invitations from Known Characters

Letters can be written from a variety of characters, which may be simple invitations, or letters to sow some seeds of disquiet. Examples include:

- Old King Cole invites the class to tea
- Max invites the children to the Land of the Wild Things
- Cinderella invites the class to the Ball on the eve of her wedding
- The Big Bad Wolf asks everyone to dinner
- A message in a bottle or on the end of balloon requests help – someone is trapped.

2   Letters which Bestow Expertise and a Role

Letters can be created in response to areas of cross curricular study. In such letters the children can be honoured as experts in the field, their skills are needed. For example, a curator at the local museum could invite renowned historians to establish a new room in the museum entitled 'Living In The Past', or a farmer might write requesting a visit from expert horticulturists as his cereal crops have failed.

3   Pamphlets which Provide Information about a Place

Genuine publicity material from a local tourist attraction (theme park, zoo, ancient building, sea life centre or water world) can be useful as a resource to start a drama session. Such pamphlets are often freely available in multiple copies and provide visual support which helps develop a sense of the place and can motivate the children to journey into this imaginary world. Tickets can be made, bags packed, the journey travelled and then on arrival, an attendant (teacher in role), could sow seeds of tension or challenge, e.g. the big wheel is not working today or the snake house is closed… !

4   Books which are Comprised of Letters

Books made up of letters can be read partly to the class, stopping at a letter which frames a problem. The class could then enter the text, inhabit the story and create further insight into the characters and the themes through their investigative drama. The children could write their own letters from the perspective of a role, reflecting upon that day's adventures before the book is continued. Such drama is useful for exploring different people's perspectives of the same event. In the case of Allan Ahlberg's *The Jolly Postman*, individual letters can be selected and used as a prompt to enter the world of traditional tales, meet some of the characters and encounter predicaments alongside them. Brian Moses' collection *Postcards from a Gnome and Other Kinds of Writing* (1993, Oxford) is an excellent drama resource with letters, adverts, postcards and diary entries all of which provide tempting snippets to explore and expand upon. We also recommend:

Ian Whybrow (1995) *Little Wolf's Book of Badness*, Collins.
Ian Whybrow (1998) *Little Wolf's Haunted Hall for Small Horrors*, Collins.
Hazel Townson (1990) *The Deathwood Letters*, Red Fox.
Herbie Brennan (1997) *Letters from a Mouse*, Walker.
Bernard Ashley (1981) 'Dear Bren', in *I'm Trying to Tell You*, Puffin.
Martina Selway (1993) *Don't Forget to Write*, Red Fox.
Janet and Allan Ahlberg (1986) *The Jolly Postman* or *Other People's Letters*, Heinemann.
Simon James (1991) *Dear Greenpeace*, Walker.

Chapter 8

MUSIC: PETER AND THE WOLF, BY PROKOFIEV

Introduction

The Russian composer Prokofiev originally composed this musical narrative for the Moscow Children's Theatre in 1936, as an introduction to the flute, the strings, the clarinet, the oboe, the bassoon and the French horn. So each character in the story is represented by one of the principal instruments of the orchestra. In this drama, the music and the story are used to prompt a dramatic exploration of the wolf's predicament.

The story begins with Peter (the strings), who lives on the edge of a Russian forest with his grandparents, taking a walk in a meadow. A little song bird (the flute) assures him that all is quiet, but when a duck (the oboe) arrives, the two birds begin to quarrel and a cat (the clarinet), prepares to pounce upon them. Peter warns the birds in time for them to escape, but is then called home by his grandfather (the bassoon), for fear of the wild wolves of the forest. No sooner have they left the meadow than a great grey wolf (the french horn), emerges from the forest to chase and eventually catch and devour the duck. Peter, who has seen all this happening from the safety of the garden, fetches a rope and ingeniously captures the wolf, using the bird as a lure. At this moment the hunters (the drums) arrive, but are persuaded by Peter not to shoot the wolf. Finally Peter leads a triumphant musical procession to the zoo with all the characters accompanying him, and even the duck from deep inside the wolf quacks!

The drama conventions highlighted in this chapter are **freeze frame**, to capture moments of action, and in contrast, **role on the wall** to build up an insightful picture of the wolf. In role on the wall, the full-size outline of a character is drawn on paper and then perceptions about this character are written on it, at various points in the drama. The music and narrative are interspersed throughout the drama to provoke imaginative possibilities, to share the essence of the tale and to create atmosphere.

Avoiding the children's suggestions and responses in order to follow the plan may mean that real opportunities for relevant learning are missed. A professional balance between teaching objectives and children's interests is always required.

Teaching Objectives and Learning Areas

- Explore wild animals, needs and rights (*the content of the drama*)
- Use and review role on the wall to examine a character (*the drama processes*)
- Develop ideas in response to the music and the narrative (*the imagination*).

Prior Experience and Materials

- No previous experience is required, but a focus on the portrayal of wolves in fiction and factual information about them would enrich the drama
- A recording of *Peter and the Wolf* by Prokofiev and a tape recorder
- Six very large sheets of lining paper and felt-tip pens.

First Encounters: Creating the Drama Context

GRANDFATHER'S WARNING

- Set the scene by introducing and describing the setting, (the countryside – forest – small house) and the characters (Peter – grandparents – animals).

- Play the opening narration and musical introduction to the instruments and the characters. Ask the children to think about how the characters might move about, and then play it again, prompting them to move about like their chosen character.

- Draw the children to you and narrate the scene inside the grandfather's house. The family are discussing the increasing number of wolves in the forest and the need for more hunters to protect humans and their domestic animals. This passage needs to evolve quickly into teacher in role as one of the grandparents, talking to the class as if they were Peter. Explain how concerned you are for his safety, you have to go into the town to sell wild mushrooms in the market, how will he look after himself? Challenge the class as Peter to respond. Can he be left alone? What will he do to make sure the animals are safe? What evidence is there you can trust him? Make explicit your concern and allude to events in your past when you escaped from wolves.

- In role, leave for the market, re-stating to the class as Peter that he must be very careful and keep the garden gate locked.

- Play the next section of music up to the point where the narrator reads '... *and locked the gate*', and the musical accompaniment ends. Depending upon the children you may wish to intersperse one or two improvisations or freeze frames into this time, prompted by the music.

Conflicts and Tensions: Developing the Drama

EXPLORING THE WOODS

- Narrate Peter leaving the house, opening the garden gate and walking into the forest. Ask the children in pairs to roleplay this briefly, with one being cautious and remembering what the grandparents said, the other being full of adventure and bravado.

- Discuss with them what children might do in the woods, e.g. build camps, make a bridge across a stream, climb trees, make rope bridges. Allow them a few minutes to improvise one of these activities.

- Continue the music and narration up to the point where the wolf has been hoisted up by the rope, the hunters want to kill it, but Peter calls out '*Don't shoot!*'

THE WOLF: WICKED OR WILD?

- In small groups, freeze-frame the trapped wolf. Ask the children to draw around one child in each group, as the wolf tied up by its tail. Provide large pieces of paper to be placed upon the floor. This outline is the basis for the role on wall. Then ask each child to individually write their thoughts about the wolf *outside* the outline of its body.

- Turn these around so that the 'tail' is at the top and either put them up on the wall at a height which can be read and added to, or move them to one side.

- Return to the children and explain you are going into role as the wolf to help them find out what she thinks. Ask them, as the hunters, to take up their guns and look at you as though you were trapped. Encourage them slowly to encircle you, narrating that no one shot the wolf, but every hunter stared at the animal. Slowly take up a position, which implies your captivity, maybe kneeling with your arms and hands behind your back, as though you were tied up, and perhaps jerking and wriggling your body as if you were trying to free yourself.

- In role as the wolf, monologue your situation: your need to live, your difficulty in finding food in the winter, your pack instinct, your own struggle to bring up your young, and the vulnerability of your pups. Perhaps suggest that you have been cut off from the rest of the pack and are searching for company, or you've lost one of your offspring. Imply your family may come to look for you and so forth. The purpose of this monologue is to offer an alternative view to the image of the wolf being a 'heartless' wild animal. Reply to any comments made and then relax and stand up.

- Suggest that the hunters begin to ask the wolf questions about her life. The children may need preparation time for this. When they are ready, retake your role, respond to their questions and continue to put your case as a wild animal with genuine needs. Try to persuade them not to shoot you.

- Ask the children to go back to their group's role on the wall, and write *inside* the body what the wolf is feeling and thinking at this moment.

Resolutions: Drawing the Drama Together

WHAT SHOULD BE DONE WITH THE WOLF?

- Ask the children to return to the circle and place all the wolf roles on the wall within it. In role as Peter, briefly appeal to them as the hunters and plead her case.

- Listen to their suggestions, argue with any you don't feel respect animals, and help the children develop their ideas and awareness of conservation and responsibility to the wild. Read out extracts from the roles in the wall and discuss the wolf's predicament, the challenge of living in the wild, the need for food and the struggle for survival.

- Together, listen to the rest of the musical narrative.

- Suggest that when Peter was in bed that night, his grandparents came to sit beside him and talk to him about the day. Invite a couple of volunteers to join you as a corporate Peter, the rest of the class can be his grandparents. Provide time for everyone to think about and discuss what they are going to say. Will

his grandparents chastise him for disobeying them? Will they understand why Peter felt he had to save the wolf? Role-play the conversation as a conclusion to the drama.

Extension Activities

- Write Peter's diary entry that night.
- Draw a story map to show the incidents leading up to the wolf's arrival. What had she been doing during the last couple of days?
- In pairs retell the events from the wolf's point of view.
- Make a poster, or a pamphlet to attract people to visit the wolf and other wild creatures in public captivity.
- Use the book *Peter and the Wolf* retold and illustrated by Ian Beck (1994, Picture Corgi), as the basis for literacy work with extracts of the music.
- Create a display with their roles on the wall, and include the storyboards and perhaps drawings of the instruments of the orchestra.

Resourcing Further Drama from Music

Music provides an evocative resource for drama and can be used in various ways. Some pieces, like Prokofiev's *Peter and the Wolf* and Delibes's *Coppelia*, represent a narrative which can be investigated. Others offer rich scope for initial dance-drama type activities which can evolve into classroom drama e.g. Grieg's *In the Hall of the Mountain King*. Alternatively such music can be used to create a sense of people and place, and prompt the teacher/class to create the predicaments which were encountered, e.g. Rimsky-Korsakov's *Flight of the Bumble Bee*. Some pieces of music provide an initial sense of the characters e.g. Saint-Saens's *The Carnival of the Animals*, which can be developed further through classroom drama. The recommendations listed below tend to be from the western classical tradition, as they are more likely to be easily obtained. However music from other cultures, such as African drumming or other genres such as rap can also be useful resources. We recommend the following:

Musorgsky, *Pictures at an Exhibition*

This involves Musorgsky walking round a gallery and describing the pictures he observes, e.g. Baba Yaga, a witch from Russian folklore, the Ballet of the Unhatched Chicks and so on. Each of the pictures could come to life and be inhabited and explored through drama.

Saint Saens, *The Carnival of the Animals*

Each movement is quite short and introduces various animals including elephants, swans, kangaroos, fish and others. Why are they celebrating? Which animals might threaten the event?

Villa Lobos, *Little Train of the Caipira*

The little mountain train sets off, gathers speed, journeys, slows, arrives and so on. Where is it going? Who might be on board? Who is waiting to welcome them? What happens on arrival?

Greig, *The Hall of the Mountain King*

A simple, but sinister repetitive tune which grows gradually faster and louder, and becomes more densely textured. There is plenty of scope here for scene setting and creating characters who dwell in the mountains. What is happening in the King's Great Hall?

Tchaikovsky, *The Nutcracker Suite*

In the nursery the toys come to life at night and dance together. But could a pause in the music herald a difficulty in the nursery? Leaving the music behind, an allegorical drama about a broken, lonely toy who cannot join in, could be developed.

Ponchielli, *Dance of the Hours*

In Disney's cartoon film *Fantasia*, this music is accompanied by a comedy ballet featuring graceless ostriches, elephants and crocodiles. It could be used to provide atmosphere for a drama set in a circus or carnival using particular extracts to build up the tension. The Disney animation could be watched as a contrast.

Chapter 9

A SHORT STORY: THE BAKERLOO FLEA BY MICHAEL ROSEN

Introduction

This drama is based on a short story which will not be read to the class until after the drama session. The idea for the setting and the roles have been borrowed from the story, which examines issues of authority and fear of the unknown in a context combining both reality and fantasy.

The story, from Michael Rosen's collection *Nasty* (1984, Penguin) provides an amusing account of some cleaning women on the Bakerloo Line of the London Underground, finding an enormous flea down one of the tunnels. Scared out of their wits, they try to involve the management, but are finally obliged to dispose of the monstrous insect through their own cunning and resources. A useful tale for drama, it offers a clear sense of the venue and the characters, yet potentially an open brief with regard to the predicament. The children can vote to select a common predicament or the teacher can lean on the story to take the drama forward. A large mutant flea, hopping about and living on detritus in the underground often appeals to children. Alternatively, their own ideas can be investigated as they seek a corporate solution to another problem of their own invention.

The drama conventions highlighted here are **whole class improvisation** in both informal and more formal contexts, and **writing/drawing in role** which has an explicit purpose and an urgency in the stressful situation in which they find themselves.

Avoiding the children's suggestions and responses in order to follow the plan may mean that real opportunities for relevant learning are missed. A professional balance between teaching objectives and children's interests is always required.

Teaching Objectives and Learning Areas
- Take part in corporate problem solving and negotiation (*personal and social skills*).
- Comment upon and discuss the figures of authority in the drama (*reflection*).
- Take the drama forward through drawing and writing in role (*the drama processes*).

Prior Experience and Materials
- No experience is necessary.
- Paper and pencils.
- A London Underground map (the largest available).

First Encounters: Creating the Drama Context

THE LONDON UNDERGROUND
- Gather the class together and discuss places where humans work underground and their experience of these e.g. mines, caves, the Channel Tunnel, and underground railway systems.
- Show them a map of the London Underground System. Explain that trains run throughout the day, but that at night at around 3 o'clock in the morning, the electric current is switched off and hundreds of cleaners descend down the stairwells to clean and clear up the rubbish left behind by commuters.

- Tell the children that you met a woman once who told you what it was like working down there, clearing up other people's rubbish. Tell them a little about her work, then invite the class to develop a drama about the London Underground.

CLEANERS ARE NEEDED

- Once general agreement has been given, move quickly into teacher as storyteller mode, and then into role as the supervisor. For example, *The group of cleaners who came to work that night as I recall, were all new to the job, so the woman in charge introduced herself: 'I'm Mrs Gordon and its good to have you join our cleaning team here on the Bakerloo Line. I believe you've all done cleaning jobs before which is very useful. Well, as we will be working together as a team, we had better get to know one another. So please introduce yourselves to each other, where have you cleaned before? I know some of you were in schools, and some of you cleaning in libraries. It's rather different here on the night shift.'*

- Let the children share their imaginary experiences, in groups of two or three, and then move on to build further belief in their role by providing imaginary uniforms and cleaning resources for them. Show them the rack in front of them, and suggest they help themselves to cleaning materials from the cupboards.

- After a few moments, stop them and ask some children what they're putting on. What did anyone find to clean with? Have they all collected bin bags, disinfectant, rubber gloves and so on?

- Back in role as the supervisor, advise them not to take their valuables just in case… hint at previous problems, *'I knew a cleaner once who, well perhaps it was just a rumour, but she said…'.* As they empty their pockets of personal possessions, ask them to show their neighbour what they are putting away for safekeeping in the lockers.

- As storyteller, narrate their descent down the stairwell to an underground station platform, lead the way, encouraging the cleaners to follow and count the first steps with you. You could prompt them to moan about their last jobs or hum tunes and finally follow in silence as you narrate the thoughts and fears of the new shift. Try to create an atmosphere of anticipation and expectation.

GETTING ON WITH THE JOB

- Once you've arrived in the tunnel, in role as the supervisor instruct the cleaners to get on with the job in hand: picking up rubbish, sweeping, mopping, washing notices and so forth.

- If they are very excited, you could help them to focus by passing out paper/pencils and asking them to draw the litter they've found. Let them show each other what they've drawn, and deal with any issues which arise in role as the supervisor. For example 'a body' might turn out to be a pile of old clothes, and could lead to a discussion on homelessness, a £20 note could be found and prompt a debate about who it belongs to…

Conflicts and Tensions: Developing the Drama

WHAT'S THAT STRANGE NOISE?

- Ask the class to take up a still position which shows them cleaning and then narrate with tension that a strange echoing noise was heard from deep within the tunnel. Tell them that some thought they recognised it, some didn't hear it at all, but those who heard it didn't like it.

- In role as the supervisor, ask the cleaners what they think that noise was? Profess to be unnerved by it, and let them share their ideas and thoughts, examples have included a ghost train, a monster, an animal escaped from a zoo, a flood, robbers trying to break into the Tower of London, prisoners from the past and aliens.

- Ask them in small groups to create freeze frames of the possible source of the noise.

- Suggest each group gives a title to their freeze frame, as if it were the accompanying headline to the photograph in a newspaper, maybe one of the cleaners had taken a camera with them.

- Observe each freeze frame together and hear their titles. As you do so link these together through narration e.g. *'Some cleaners imagined the noise was a train derailed in the distant past, others believed that…'*.

- At this point, in order to have a common direction, either vote together to agree the source of the noise, or offer Michael Rosen's idea of the giant flea. You could read an extract from the story to add detail. Decide together upon the source of the noise and the problem.

HELP! WHAT SHOULD WE DO?

- Discuss briefly with the children what they think the cleaners would do in such a situation with a giant flea, ghost train or whatever down the tunnel. This conversation is in preparation for a whole class improvisation.

- In role as the supervisor, begin the improvisation, call for action, share your own concerns and encourage the children to make suggestions and identify the possible consequences of their ideas. Avoid the group splitting up at all costs, but if some are absolutely determined to fight, narrate the possibility that a few cleaners ventured down the tunnel but didn't return, the class could call out their fictional names together. So the group still have to decide what action to take.

- Honour their decision, and improvise accordingly. At some point it is likely they'll seek help and/or go to inform others of the problem. At this point narrate their long weary ascent up the stairs.

- Ask one child to continue leading the cleaners up the stairwell and take up a new role as the duty manager, reading and filling in forms in your office. Narrate that at the top of the stairs, the cleaners reached the manager's office and that through the glass door they could see the boss.

- As silence descends, carry on with your work and wait for the class to take the initiative to make their concerns clear to the management.

WILL ANYONE BELIEVE US?

- In role as manager of the night shift, respond to their concerns brusquely and authoritatively, but try to establish the facts. Your attitude needs to contrast with that of the supervisors: ask questions to elucidate details – suggest incredulity – disbelief – are they hallucinating? Surely they've not left their jobs below just because of a simple noise? Deny all knowledge of any previous rumours and stories. This whole class improvisation may become quite heated if you refuse to believe them.

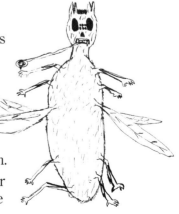

Mahdi (aged 7)

- As the manager, demand evidence in the form of pictures or labelled diagrams of what they think they saw. This might serve to convince you and help establish what can be done.

- Ask small groups to improvise a scene in which the boss is taken down the tunnel by the workers to hear or see the problem. Watch a few together.

Resolutions: Drawing the Drama Together

SEEKING SOLUTIONS

- Back in role as the duty manager, in a whole class improvisation, apologise for not believing them and, request their help. Try to ingratiate yourself with them now that you need their help. Do they have any ideas about how to solve the problem? Share your concern that thousands of commuters will be coming down the underground very shortly. Discuss the possible options together.

Patrick (aged 6)

- During this improvisation, answer the phone and conduct a one sided conversation with your boss. Tentatively explain the urgent situation; there are hundreds of other cleaners who must be got to safety, station entrances must be manned to warn commuters, connecting trains cannot be allowed to stop and so on. Tell your boss you'll come up with a solution as soon as possible.

- Urge the class to write their suggestions quickly and write one yourself. Let the class share their plans by reading them to one another. Leave the ending open, but as their storyteller relate that although a solution was found, you never found out exactly what it was.

- Reflect upon the drama by considering the different authority/leadership roles they encountered; the duty manager and the supervisor. Prompt the children to give examples from the drama as they discuss how these figures behaved, their motives, views, roles and responsibilities in the organisation.

I am the rat catcher. I won't let that flea be killed. He is not a harmful creature, he's a nice animal, he'll feed on all the rats and dead mice, so chuck them down the hole and he will LIVE. Nobody can kill him, I won't let them. He lives down that tunnel and he can stay there, it's his home and we must stop thinking of ways to get rid of him and let him *live*.
Don't keep talking about ideas to trap him, we'll just have to take up the train track and when the track and the trains are out the way, then we'll drain the electricity and give it to somebody who is poor and then they'll have enough for … 20 years. This is Professor Anthony talking, and I'll tell you something, I work as rat catcher and if you have rat problems, tell me about them and I'll get rid of them for you by giving them to the flea. Rats eat cheese, they spread poision and disease around and they also … cause a lot of trouble.
So we need that flea we *really* do.

I want the flea to LIVE. Nobody can stop him. I am the rat catcher, I think the flea must! be allowed to LIVE!

Anthony (aged 6)

58

- Consider how this problem in the Underground was sorted out. Discuss other situations they've encountered in which negotiation and discussion were essential to reach a solution.

Extension Activities

- Write newspaper articles about the flea, (or ghost train/whatever).
- Role play interviews with the press to encourage retelling of the tale.
- Make tape recordings of chosen parts of the drama. Listen to a couple as a class and discuss the language used by those in positions of authority.
- Make a class zigzag book to retell their tale. Encourage the children to take this home to retell or read to their parents.
- Read '*The Bakerloo Flea*' by Michael Rosen to the children – discuss the differences, defend their ideas and their story line as a valid alternative. Use the story for other literacy work.

Resourcing Further Drama from Short Stories

Short stories, like many of the picture books and traditional tales mentioned in this book, provide good resource material for initiating and framing drama. The story provides the people, place or predicament, or some combination of these, and frames the dramatic action which seeks to examine the issues arising in the tale. Short stories can be used in a variety of ways. Books which offer semi-independent chapters about the main characters can also be useful.

1   **Taking the Short Story as a Guide**

   Read the story/chapter and stop occasionally to allow the children to step into the text and find out more about the themes, characters and issues in the story. After some dramatic exploration, the next few paragraphs can be read and then the motives, attitudes and inner concerns of the characters examined through drama. The story guides the drama and provides a structure, and the drama enriches the language of the unsaid in the tale.

2   **Building Drama from an Extract**

   One section of the short story/chapter can be read. This will leave lots of unanswered questions and if it presents an interesting conflict or some ambiguous, yet intriguing knowledge then the class can build their drama upon this.

3   **Creating a Follow Up Tale**

   Having read the complete story/chapter to the class, a new story/next chapter can be created with the same characters (as well as new ones) in another venue. The class can shape this drama more fully for themselves, co-authoring a new short story in action which examines alternative themes, but builds upon their knowledge of the particular characters and their relationships.

We recommend the following short stories and short story collections:

Joan Aitken (1968) *A Necklace of Raindrops*, Puffin.
Bernard Ashley (1992) *More Stories from Dockside School*, Walker.
Bernard Ashley (1981) *I'm Trying to Tell You*, Puffin.
Betty Byars (1993) *The Seven Treasure Hunts*, Red Fox.
Jamila Gavin (1979) *The Magic Orange Tree and Other Stories*, Magnet.
Shirley Hughes (1996) *Stories by Firelight*, Walker.
Julia Jarman (1995) *The Jessame Stories*, Mammoth.
Terry Jones (1981) *Fairy Tales*, Puffin.
George Layton (1981) *The Fib and Other Stories*, Lion.
Michael Morpurgo (1998) *Red Eyes at Night*, Hodder Headline.
Philippa Pearce (1986) *The Lion at School and Other Stories*, Puffin.
Alf Prøysen (1995) *Mrs Pepperpot in the Magic Wood*, Puffin.
Jill Tomlinson (1968) *The Owl who was Afraid of the Dark*, Young Puffin.

THE BAKERLOO FLEA, BY MICHAEL ROSEN

Not long ago I was in a pub round the Elephant & Castle, and I got talking to a woman, an oldish woman. And we were talking about this and that, and she said she used to be a cleaner down the Underground. I didn't know, but it seems as if every night after the last tube, they switch the electric current off and teams of night-cleaners go through the Underground, along the tunnels, cleaning up all the muck, rubbish, fag ends and stuff that we chuck on to the lines. They sweep out between the lines on one station, and then, in a gang of about six or seven, walk on to the next station along the lines in the tunnels.

Anyway, this woman (I don't know her name), she says to me:

'Did you ever hear talk of the Bakerloo flea?'

'Bakerloo flea?' I said. 'No, no, never.'

'Well,' she said, 'you know there are rats down there – down the underground? Hundreds of 'em. And the thing is,' she said, 'is that some of them have grown enormous. Huge great big things.'

'I've heard of them,' I said. 'Super rats.'

'Right,' she says. 'Now you tell me,' she says, 'what lives on rats? Fleas, right?

Fleas. So – the bigger the rats the bigger the fleas. Stands to reason. These rats, they feed on all the old garbage that people throw down on the lines. It's amazing what people throw away, you know.'

She told me they found a steak down there once, lipstick, a bowler hat, beads, a box of eggs and hundreds and hundreds of sweets – especially Maltesers and those balls of bubble gum you get out of slot machines.

Anyway, the rats eat these, get big, and it seems that one day they were working the Bakerloo Line – Elephant & Castle to Finchley Road – and just before Baker Street one of the women in the gang was looking ahead, and she screamed out:

'Look – look – what's that?' Up in front was a great, grey, spiky thing with huge hairy legs and big jaws. It was as big as a dog – bigger.

And the moment she screamed, it jumped away from them, making a sort of grating, scraping noise. Well, they were scared stiff. Scared stiff. But they had to finish the job, so they carried on up the line to Finchley Road. But they didn't see it again that night or the next, or the next.

Some of them thought they'd imagined it, because it can get very spooky down there. They sing and shout a lot she told me, and tell saucy jokes, not fit for my ears.

Anyway, about a fortnight later, at the same place – just before Baker Street on the Bakerloo Line – one of them looks up and there it was again. A great, big, grey, spiky thing with long legs and big jaws.

'It's a flea, sure to God it's a flea,' one of them said.

The moment it heard this, again it jumped. Again, they heard this scraping, grating sound, and it disappeared down the tunnel – in the dark. They walked on, Baker Street, St. John's Wood, Swiss Cottage, to Finchley Road. Nothing.

Anyway – this time they had a meeting. They decided it *was* a flea, a gigantic flea, and it must have grown up from a family of fleas that had lived for years and years growing bigger and bigger, sucking the blood of all the fat rats down there.

So they decided that it was time to tell one of the high-ups in London Transport or they wouldn't go down there any more.

For a start off, no one'd believe them.

'Just a gang of women seeing things in the dark,' the supervisor said.

Right! One of them had a bright idea. She said:

'I'll tell you what we'll do – we'll tell them that we're coming out on strike, and we'll tell the papers about the flea, the Bakerloo flea. It'll be a huge scandal – no one'll dare go by tube, it'll be a national scandal.'

So they threatened the manager with this, and this time the high-ups really moved. They were so scared the story might get out, and they'd be blamed, and one of *them* would lose their jobs.

So for a start they stopped all cleaning on the Bakerloo Line, and one of the high-ups went down the tunnel with the women. You can just see it, can't you? Four in the morning, a gang of six women with feather dusters, and one of the bowler hat and briefcase brigade walking down the tunnel on the hunt for the Bakerloo flea. Sounded incredible to me.

Anyway, it seems as if they came round that same corner just before Baker Street and the women had gone quiet and the bloke was saying: 'If this is a hoax, if this is a trick...' when they heard that awful, hollow, scraping noise.

At first they couldn't see it, but then – there it was – not *between* the lines this time – *on* the lines – a gigantic flea. No question, that's what it was.

Well, he took one look at it, and next moment he was backing off.

'Back, ladies, back, back, ladies!'

Of course *he* was more scared than they were. Terrified. But he was even more terrified when one of the women let out this scream. Not because *she* was was scared, but to scare off the flea. And it worked. It jumped. Right out of sight.

Well there was no carrying on up the line that night.

'Back, ladies, back,' was all he could say, and back they went.

Next thing they knew, they were all called into an office with a carpet and the Queen on the wall. And there was a whole gang of these men.

First thing, one of them says, they weren't to let anyone know of this, no one at all must ever hear of what they had all seen. There was no point in letting a panic develop. Anyway, next he says:

'We haven't let the grass grow under our feet. We've got a scientist with us.'

And then the scientist, he says:

'I've got this powder. Deadly flea powder. All you need to do is spread this up and down the Bakerloo Line, and there'll be no more trouble with this flea thing.'

Well, the woman in the pub – I never found out her name – said:

'So who's going to spread this stuff about down there? The Army?'

'No,' the man said. 'We don't see any need for that. You,' he says, 'you.'

'So that's a fine one,' the woman said to me. 'First of all they said it was just a bunch of women afraid of the dark, then they send Tarzan in pinstripes down there and he can't get out fast enough, and now it's us that has to spread this flea powder.'

'Well,' she said, 'we knew it wouldn't be any good anyway. Flea powder never is.'

They took it down there, threw it about between Regents Park and Baker Street and Swiss Cottage – while up above, in the big houses, ambassadors from all over the world slept soundly in their beds. They told them not to go down for a week, and not to breathe a word of it to anyone.

'They were more scared of a story in the papers than we were of the flea,' she said.

It hadn't attacked anyone, no one had seen it there in daytime, so down they went. But there it was again – sitting there just before Baker Street, with some of the powder sticking to the hairs on its legs. But this time, instead of hopping away down the line, it turned and faced them. They turned and ran, and then it leaped. It leaped at the women, and they ran back down the tunnel to Regent's Park. This great, grey flea was trying to get at them.

'We screamed,' she said, 'we really screamed, but it was after us, 'cos you see that damned flea powder hadn't killed the flea – it had killed the rats. It was starving for fresh blood. Probably *mad* for blood, by now,' she said. 'We ran and ran and the flea was hopping – but it was hitting the roof of the tunnel, it was so mad to get at us. There was this terrible scraping sound of its shell on the roof of the tunnel, and it'd fall back onto the lines. So we could move faster than it. We rushed back to Regent's Park, and calls went up and down the line and all over the system to lock the gates on every station and seal the system. Seal off the Underground system of London. Well, it was about four o'clock – two hours to go before a million people would be down there.

'What were they going to do? Upstairs in the office they were in a blind panic. They could've done something about it earlier, instead of fobbing us off. They couldn't call in the Army without telling the Minister, and if they told the Minister, he'd tell the Prime Minister, and all the high-ups would get the sack. So they had this plan to turn the current on, and run the maintenance train at high speed through the tunnel from Finchley Road to the Elephant and Castle, in the hope that it would get killed beneath the wheels of the train, or smashed against the buffers at the Elephant.

'They did it. They sent it through. Of course *that* didn't work. We knew it wouldn't work. Anyone that's lived with a flea knows you can't squash fleas – you've got to crack 'em. They're hard, rock hard.'

After the maintenance man ran the maintenance train through, they went down to the gates at Regent's Park, and they stood and listened, and from down below they could hear the grating, scraping noise of its shell on its legs. Of course, it was obvious now why it had stuck to this stretch of the line all the time. Some of the juiciest rubbish was in the bins round those posh parts, so you got the biggest rats, so that was where you got the great Bakerloo flea.

So now they had less than two hours to get rid of the flea, or leave it for a day and run the risk of letting a million people down into the tunnels to face a flea, starving, starving for blood, or shutting the whole system down and telling everyone to go by bus.

'Well you know what happened?' she said. '*We* did it. We got rid of it.'

'You did?'

'Yes, we did it.'

'Vera's old man worked on the dustcarts for Camden Council. She knew how to kill the flea. It was Vera's plan that what we'd do was go down, actually down onto the line at Oxford Circus with dustbin lids, banging them with brushes and broom handles, and drive the flea back up the line to Finchley Road where the Bakerloo Line comes out of the tunnel into the open air. And at Finchley Road,

Vera's old man and his gang would have a couple of carts backed up into the tunnel. And that's what we did. We got driven to Vera's place to get her old man up, on to his mates' places to get them up, then they went to the Council builders' yard to get boards, builders' planks. We got the lids off the bins, and down we went. Oxford Circus, Regent's Park, Baker Street, St. John's Wood, Swiss Cottage, Finchley Road, and we shouted every step of the way.

'We saw it just once at Swiss Cottage waiting for us, but we walked together holding the lids up in front of us like shields, and it was as if we knew it couldn't get at us this time, 'cos it turned – it had just room to turn in the tunnel – and as we came up to Finchley Road still banging and shouting, it leaped – not at us, but at one of the carts. Alongside it was the other one, between the wheels were the boards, some of them stacked up to block off all the gaps. The flea was trapped between us with our lids and the back of the dustcarts. It leaped, hit the roof of the tunnel, just like it did when it chased us. We shouted and banged. It leaped again. This time we had it. It was in the back of the dustcart.

'We kept up the banging and the shouting. We got as near to the back of the dustcart as we could. We could see it there, every hair of its legs, and Vera shouts:

'Turn it on, Bob, turn it on,' and Bob turned on the masher (they call it 'The Shark'), in the back of his cart. And it bit into the back of that flea like giant nails crunching through eggshells. The smell was revolting. Bit by bit, the flea was dragged into the cart. We could see it as it went: first its body, then its legs. I'll never forget the sight of those huge hairy legs twitching about in the back of Bob's cart, Vera shouting:

'You've got him, love, you've got him!'

'He had, too, that was that. That was the end of the Bakerloo flea. But do you know, when we got up to the top, that load from head office were there. They were crying, crying out of relief, crying their eyes out. Twenty minutes later, hundreds and thousands of people were down there, off to work, none the wiser. They didn't know about any flea, any Bakerloo flea. They don't even know we go down there every night cleaning up their mess for them. Of course, head office made us promise never to breathe a word of it. We promised.

Vera said:

'What's it worth to you?'

He said:

'Your honour. Your word. And your word's your honour.'

'And they gave us a week's extra holiday tagged on to August Bank Holiday that year.'

She told me I was the first person she'd ever told the story to, and told me never to tell anyone. The scandal would be terrible. I don't know whether to believe her or not.

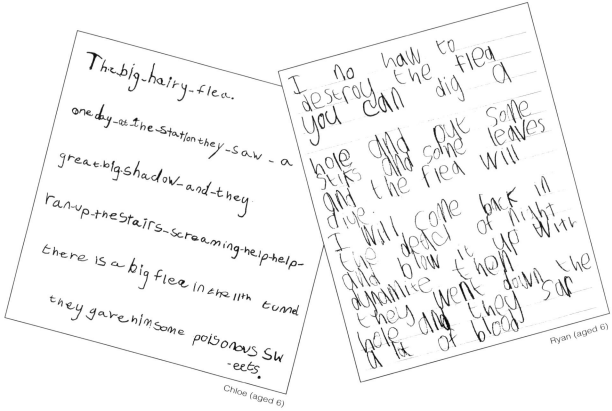

The big hairy flea.

one day at the station they saw a

great big shadow and they

ran up the stairs screaming help help

there is a big flea in the 11th tunnel

they gave him some poisonous sw-eets.

Chloe (aged 6)

I no haw to destroy the flea you can dig a hole and sum stiks and some leaves and the flea will dive. I will come back in the dead of night and blow it up with dynamite they went down the hole and they sor a lit of blood

Ryan (aged 6)

Chapter 10

SCIENTIFIC KNOWLEDGE: THE BUTTERFLY FARM

INSECTS EVERYWHERE !

Help needed urgently. An inexperienced gardener cannot deal with the insect population overtaking her garden. Only environmentally friendly experts should apply.

Contact: **Mrs Greentown**

Tel: 01227 982341

Introduction

This drama is resourced and supported by the children's knowledge about minibeasts. The dramatic exploration provides a trigger for research about butterflies: their feeding, habitat, breeding and species variety. The information gathered through science work is used in the drama sessions which in themselves prompt further scientific investigation, so the drama feeds the research and vice versa.

The project involves the class responding to an advertisement in the local paper requesting help from insect experts. Mrs Greentown has recently moved out of the city, her garden is deluged with caterpillars and she needs advice. She decides to recruit some entomologists to assist her in finding out about butterfly needs, to build a safe habitat for them and eventually open a Butterfly Farm. Over the weeks that follow, various problems befall the team of experts, including an angry lettuce farmer whose crop is being eaten, and a butterfly collector who would like to buy butterflies to impale and mount them. The need to address these challenges, open the Farm, and educate the visiting public, prompt the research and investigation. This works well as a class project over several weeks, since establishing the Farm in the classroom can involve considerable art and design work as well as music and English. It can be integrated within a non-fiction literacy focus, involving the production of information texts.

The drama convention explicitly employed in this drama is **mantle of the expert**, which casts the children in the role of experts and prompts them to use their knowledge and extend their expertise. Their knowledge is respected and new problems challenge them to develop it further.

Avoiding the children's suggestions and responses in order to follow the plan may mean that real opportunities for relevant learning are missed. A professional balance between following the teaching objectives and the children's interests is always required.

Teaching Objectives and Learning Areas

- Research the butterfly species, their environment, lifecycle and habitat (*the content of the drama*)
- Employ language to report and persuade (*language*)
- Use the responsibility of mantle of the expert (*the drama processes*).

Prior Experience and Materials

- It is essential that the class has worked on minibeasts (but not butterflies) prior to this drama, as this will enable them to take on the mantle of expertise as entomologists. The drama represents an extension of the science curriculum work, with a specific focus upon butterflies.

- Stick the advertisement into a copy of your local paper or Adscene
- Reference texts for science work on butterflies
- Clipboards for their work as entomologists/scientists
- A large rose spray
- A plain shoebox
- An easel and paper
- Ribbon or crepe paper for the opening ceremony.

First Encounters: Creating the Drama Context

SOMEONE NEEDS OUR EXPERTISE

- Put out your drama symbol (see p.97) and draw the children's attention to the advert placed in the local paper. Ask them, as experts on insects, if they want to answer the advertisement and offer help? Suggest you ring the number to make enquiries.

- With the children calling out the number, ring Mrs Greentown and hold a one-sided conversation with her. Cover your hand over the mouthpiece and tell the children she is asking what they know about caterpillars and insects, she's got a lot of caterpillars in her garden and is at her wits' end, could they find the time to visit and give advice? Reassure Mrs Greentown that you have been working with the scientists for some weeks, and that you know they are very knowledgeable about minibeasts, you feel sure they'll be able to help. Take down her address.

- Suggest everyone packs a bag of relevant equipment ready for the visit, discuss what might prove useful, e.g. magnifying glasses, tweezers, cameras. Ask the class to tell each other what they are putting in their bags. Give real clipboards and pencils to each young scientist for recording purposes.

- Narrate walking down the streets, out of town into the countryside (or catching the bus), prompting the children to physically journey with you. The narration needs to stress the changing environmental features.

- On arrival, comment on the farming land all around Mrs Greentown's home, Papillon Cottage, and suggest someone rings the bell.

INSECTS GALORE

- In role as Mrs Greentown, welcome the class as the experts who've answered her advertisement, and take them into the garden, briefly commenting upon features in it, to help the children picture it in their imaginations, and then explain your predicament. You've recently moved from the city, know little about gardening and are now beset with caterpillars and other insects. You just don't know what to do with them. Let some discussion begin, but soon suggest the scientists might like to examine the insects, before making their recommendations.

- Let the class improvise; observing, examining, counting and collecting some of the insect pupae and caterpillars. Suggest they each draw an insect they've found. Remain in role, talking to individuals about your concerns as they investigate and use their equipment. 'Photographs' might also be taken.

- Draw the scientists together to sit down on your patio and ask for information about what they have found. Let them share their work and then discuss what can be done since you don't wish to spray the caterpillars, but they are devouring everything in sight – your flowers, vegetables and so on. Throughout, express your lack of knowledge and defer to their views. At some point in this discussion, comment that if the butterflies which emerge are as interesting and beautiful as they suggest, you'd like other people to enjoy them. You wonder, if you used part of your big garden, could they provide the insect expertise and help you create a special Butterfly Farm?

- Ask the class in pairs to generate ideas for the Farm.

- Together draw a provisional plan of the Butterfly Farm, including the positioning of possible walk-though netted-frames, a pupae area, the open garden, a shop, parking and so on.

- Thank them for their labours and ask them to meet you a week later, to inform you about the environmental conditions and feeding arrangements necessary for caterpillars and butterflies. Perhaps incubators will be needed? You will need their advice and more information to establish a really safe habitat.

Research Work

When it is appropriate within the curriculum, re-establish with the children the research questions which need to be answered in preparation for their site meeting next week at Papillon Cottage. Undertake this investigation, using reference texts, CD-ROMs and other resources as appropriate. The key areas at present are environment and feeding. Whilst this work is being undertaken prompt conversations about the Butterfly Farm.

Laura (aged 7)

Conflicts and Tensions: Developing the Drama

THE SITE MEETING

- In role as Mrs Greentown, open the meeting, show them the plan and update them on your application to the local council, who at least on the telephone seem positive about the project. Perhaps refer briefly to the café plans and then focus on their scientific knowledge. List the information offered under headings and ask questions regarding the consequences for the Farm. What materials need to be purchased e.g. glass, gauze, a pond, heat, plants. Together evaluate and discuss the relative use of such resources.

- Explain that you find it hard to imagine the actual butterfly house, can they physically make it with their bodies, as a kind of model? What features will they place where? Do this as a whole class freeze frame and briefly ask questions about what part of the greenhouse they individually represent.

- Gather together for a tea break to draw a single bird's eye view of the butterfly house itself. While one child is adding a feature to the plan, comment that you want to fetch a book and that you'll just be a minute or two. Walk well away from the group.

TROUBLE WITH THE NEIGHBOURS

- Knock loudly and assertively at the door and, brandishing a plant spray, re-enter as Mr Soil. Angrily march into the room and make your views and exasperation clear. You've been trying to eradicate insects from your farm for years and now you've lost some of your lettuces due to a recent increase in caterpillars, probably originating from this property. Your view is that insects are no use to anyone, and need to be eradicated. You expect they've got spray guns too in their garden sheds at home, because insects just cause trouble, bees sting people, flies spread dirt, butterflies are feeble looking and so on. Let this tirade against insects move into questioning e.g. Why are they here? Are they going to cause more trouble? Do they agree insects are just a nuisance? Improvise this fairly briefly with the class.

- Set up a piece of forum theatre, to examine the issues and the personal interaction between you as Mr Soil and the scientists. Enter again and meet a small group of children as the scientists. Let the rest of the class observe the improvisation and stop the drama occasionally, they can advise their fellow scientists about some of the positive features of insects (e.g. honey, pollination, beauty, keeping aphids under control). This should help the small group defend their position as well as manage communication with this unreasonable individual. Close the forum theatre by leaving, stating that you'll put up with the situation for three short months, but they'd better get their insects under control or under cover, or else you'll return with your spray gun.

- Return as Mrs Greentown, with a book and ask the children what all the shouting was about? Use the opportunity for the class to re-articulate the major points of their arguments and reflect upon them. Discuss whether their arrangements will be adequate to control the insects and address Mr Soil's concerns.

- Show the class your reference book on colourful butterflies and suggest that Mr Soil and others may not know how many different fabulous species exist. Request that they research the various kinds, including the night flying moths, and report back to you. By next week's meeting, the builders should have completed constructing the butterfly house and you will order the various incubated pupae they recommend in their reports.

Research Work

Establish small groups of children to become the experts on various kinds of butterfly: red admirals, cabbage whites and so on. Provide time and resources for the groups to produce reports on their particular butterfly, including information on size, specific features, habitat, food and so on. Any necessary adaptations to the butterfly house will also need to be noted. Ongoing artwork could by now be transforming the classroom, or an area in it, into the butterfly house. During their research work, take receipt of a letter from Mrs Greentown one morning. You could produce a copy of the letter, for each group to read for themselves. This explains that their scientific reports will need to be ready to be presented to some visitors, as she's invited photographers and local journalists to the next site meeting. This is an early move towards marketing the Butterfly Farm as a worthwhile tourist/ecological attraction. Encourage each group to work as a team and provide preparation and rehearsal time for their presentation at the informal press conference. This could involve showing any artwork, models, and diagrams as well as information on their particular kind of butterfly.

Beth (aged 7)

Conflicts and Tensions: Developing the Drama

A STRANGER AT THE PRESS CONFERENCE

- Set up the press conference and begin their presentations. In role as Mrs Greentown, with several of your team, you could outline the overall scheme and let each group inform the audience about a butterfly species which they believe should be in the Farm. Groups not presenting can sit in the press seats and ask questions in role as journalists/visitors. Personally, after introducing the Farm, join the journalists and prompt questions from there.

- In a break between two of the later presentations, narrate the arrival of a stranger who is carrying a plain cardboard box. In role as this butterfly collector, ask questions about where you can acquire butterflies, play a slightly ominous mysterious role. You agree they are beautiful, indeed people will pay good money for tropical specimens in good condition. Don't reveal your identity or business interest, but respond to their comments or questions in role and leave, suggesting you'll return another day.

- In role as Mrs Greentown, close the meeting, thank the scientists for their informed reports about the butterflies to be stocked and tell the press that soon the publicity pamphlets and posters will be released, copies of which you will send them. You trust that all the local papers will write positive reports about the forthcoming Butterfly Farm. Ask if anyone knows anything about the mysterious individual who left early?

- Suggest that many of the scientists spoke to each other on the phone that evening. They were suspicious of the person who'd asked lots of questions, was he/she really a journalist? How could their butterflies be protected from such people? In pairs, role play these telephone conversations and share some snippets of them.

Jessica (aged 7)

Research Work

Prepare information for the grand opening of the Butterfly Farm. Produce publicity leaflets or posters, and small information resumés about the various stages in the life cycle of butterflies and so on. Their resumés could be polypocketed or laminated as information cards for visitors to read as tour guides. Diagrams of the butterfly house and details of the functions of each room could also be made and notices and labels created. Newspaper articles could be written and a song and/or butterfly life cycle dance could be created. You might make invitations and invite another class or parents to the grand opening of the Butterfly Farm.

Resolutions: Drawing the Drama Together

THE GRAND OPENING

- Arrange with the children a ceremonial and ritualised opening, in which there are allotted places, the presentation of ribbons, the cutting of a tape and the symbolic release of two rare butterflies into the space by the dignitary who is going to open the farm. This person could be you in role, or a child who you know can give the role some stature.

- Follow this with a song or dance, and then let the scientists take their visitors (the other class or parents), on a tour around the Farm. All the work from this project can be displayed, with sections in the butterfly house allocated to various kinds of butterflies and the classroom literally transformed for the occasion.

- Evaluate the project with the class. What were the highlights? What challenges did they overcome? How was this different from other science work?

Extension Activities

- Further work on drama and related research could focus on animal predators, protection, camouflage and the need to facilitate breeding in the Farm. A dead butterfly could be found ensnared in a spider's web, mysterious deaths might occur, or birds could find their way into the netted butterfly house. All such challenges have consequences for the Farm and prompt the need for further knowledge.

- The children's own non-fiction reference texts on the different kinds of butterflies could be published, complete with indexes, contents and glossaries.

- Non-narrative texts on insects, or the life cycle of a butterfly could be used for related literacy work.

- Real live pupae (as well as other relevant reference material) can be ordered from **Insect Lore** in Milton Keynes. Their brochure also offers quality insect puppets. (Tel: 01908 200 794)

- Art and craftwork could include work on symmetry, tessellations and collages as well as producing promotional materials such as badges, T-shirt printing or posters.

- The role play area could be the Butterfly Farm café and shop with appropriate menus, décor and its own problems, such as plumbing, the chef's absence and so on.

This book is fantastic and superb. The close up drawings are very detailed. If you want to know anything about the small white, small tortoiseshell, Peacock and Brimstone butterflies. This is the book to get!

Resourcing Further Drama from Scientific Knowledge

Many science investigations can be enriched by placing them within an imaginary dramatic context. Dorothy Heathcote's drama work on the mantle of the expert can be usefully integrated into common themes such as the human body, materials, the senses and sound. The mantle of expertise is worn by the children, and their knowledge is tapped and developed through involvement in some corporate business venture. The venture is investigated through a number of dramatic engagements which sustain the children's interest and provide a purpose for the extension of their knowledge. Examples might include:

1   **A food project:** the children could become nutritionists and establish a healthy eating café, and offer educational talks in local schools. Difficulties might include hygiene checks, food poisoning, or competition from other organic cafés.

2   **A project on space:** the children could become astronomers and set up a new observatory or space station. Numerous challenges might beset such a project, the variability of the weather, broken machinery, asteroids or visitors from outer space.

3   **A project on our bodies and keeping healthy:** the children could become psychologists, physiotherapists or beauticians and create a local Keep Fit Centre with indoor and outdoor facilities. Problems might include muscle strain, an allergic reaction to facial cream, or attracting the clientele from a lethargic local community.

4   **A project on materials:** the children could become clothes designers, testing fabric elasticity, tie-dyeing materials, mixing colours and weaving to prepare for their educational fashion show, in which fashions are modelled and information about the fabrics is provided. Challenges might include the work of plagiarists, and competition from other fashion houses, as well as stolen designs or difficult models.

Chapter 11

A FAITH TALE: RAMA AND SITA

Rama and the Demon King

An Ancient Tale from India

Jessica Souhami

Introduction

This drama uses as its source the Hindu faith tale of 'The Ramayana', which is part of the origin of Divali, the Hindu Festival of Light. It contains many stories within it, but only a couple are investigated in the drama described below. So the potential exists to extend the drama and find out more through reading, storytelling and further dramatic exploration of other stories within the epic. The story chosen for this drama causes the battle between Prince Rama and the demon King Ravana. It is read or told first, and then particular moments in the story are revisited and expanded to enrich the children's understanding of the chosen issues of good, evil and altruism. There are parallels here with the temptation of Adam and Eve.

The tale tells how two gods, Rama and Sita, lived in human form in a forest with Lakshmana, Rama's loyal half brother, although Prince Rama was heir to a great kingdom. His stepmother had beguiled his father into banishing him for fourteen years. Whilst in the forest, the sister of the demon King Ravana tries to seduce Rama away from his wife Sita but fails. Angry at her rejection, the demon's sister insists her brother attacks Prince Rama. Clever Ravana, (who has twenty arms and ten heads with long yellow fangs and eyes like burning fires), sends a beautiful golden deer to tempt Sita. In fact the deer is a transformed demon shaped to deceive and lure. The trick works, Rama and Lakshmana chase after it to capture it for Sita, who is left alone and vulnerable. The terrible King Ravana kidnaps Sita, carrying her off in his chariot to his island of hell, Lanka, where she is held prisoner. However, Hanuman, the white monkey, helps Rama and Lakshmana search for Sita with battalions of monkeys and bears, and eventually she is found.

Hanuman visits her and promises to bring his animal army to rescue her and fight the evil demons on Lanka. A long battle ensues which involves many acts of bravery, but finally Rama defeats the evil Ravana and rescues his wife, Sita. They return to their own country to be welcomed back with oil lamps lit in every home and rule peacefully thereafter.

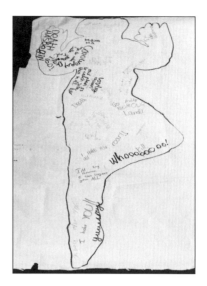

One drama convention highlighted in this chapter is **role on the wall**. In this a role/character is represented in picture form, (often by a large outline or drawing) and information about the person concerned is written on this. Additional statements or knowledge about the person can be added as the drama progresses, and further perspectives recorded at the close of the drama. **Thought-tracking** is also used to help the children give voice to the thoughts of various characters, exploring their views and perspectives at various points in the drama.

Avoiding the children's suggestions and responses in order to follow the plan may mean that real opportunities for relevant learning are missed. A professional balance between teaching objectives and children's interests is always required.

Teaching Objectives and Learning Areas

- Consider and discuss the concepts of good, evil and altruism (*reflection*)
- Explore the meaning of the Hindu faith tale, the Ramayana (*the content of the drama*)
- Adapt successfully to whole class/small group/individual work (*personal and social skills*).

Prior Experience and Materials

- None is necessary, although this work would fit well within a focus on Hindu culture or an examination of different faith tales. Literary work on characters, their morals, behaviour and attitudes would also provide a context for this drama
- 12 large sheets of paper/lining paper and felt pens
- Two used birthday cards
- A drum.

First Encounters: Creating the Drama Context

THE TALE AND ITS CHARACTERS

- Read or tell a fairly brief version of the Ramayana to the class, e.g. You could use the big book *Rama and the Demon King* by Jessica Souhami (1997, Frances Lincoln). It needs to include the key elements of the tale as described above.

> What would it be like to be one of those evil spirits?
> Teacher

> Horrible
> Leon

- Tell the children you are going to focus on the good and evil in the tale, and ask them to talk to their neighbour about the examples of evil in the tale.
- Make two lists with the class of the good and evil characters in the tale, and create a hierarchy of them in relation to their relative importance in the story.

> It might be a bit scary 'cos you might think you'd get killed as they are always fighting
> Jade
> (8 year olds)

- Suggest small groups create a statue of the demon King Ravana and shout out words and phrases, as well as make sounds or noises epitomising this evil character.

Conflicts and Tensions: Developing the Drama

LIFE ON THE ISLAND OF HELL

- Describe and narrate life on the island of Lanka, a place where Ravana treats all his demons as mere servants, and they in turn trust no one. The demons tell tales and lies, and make fun of one another, so tension and conflict are rife, and greed and competition are the prevailing principles.

- Pair the children up as Ravana and a servant, and ask them to improvise the tyrannical master ordering the demon about. After a couple of minutes change their roles over.

- In role as Ravana, call all your demons together (the whole class) and tell them you're both disappointed and angry that certain spirits have been breaking your rules. You have found incriminating evidence against some of them, in their rooms. At this point produce the evidence: two birthday cards. Carefully show them and slowly, with great deliberation, rip them up, all the time reinforcing your power and the negative values of the island. Go on to tell them you are displeased that so many of the humans are also helping one another, and that the time has come to change the humans' friendly ways.

- Tell the demons that to prove their worth and achieve your plan, they will be tested. First they must turn themselves into animals and you will judge which creature they are. Ask the children to take up still positions and decide on which animal they're going to be. Beat the drum rhythmically, and let them move on each beat gradually changing into an animal.

- Ask the animals to show movements which will tempt humans to follow them.

- Turn this into a competition in keeping with the spirit of the island. Divide the class in two and form a circle with half the class. Inside the circle the other half move about as an animal, for you to judge the most effective 'lure'. Suggest to them that since this is a place of whisperers and gossips, any of the sitting watching demons can come up to you during the displays and whisper some gossipy comment about anyone in the ring into your ear. Make sure you see both halves.

- In role as Ravana, tell them none of their lures has been chosen for the special task of tricking Rama away from Sita, but you will turn one of their number into a beautiful and graceful deer with sleek skin and golden horns for this task. The rest are to go out into the world to begin to tempt and corrupt mankind.

WHEN EVIL IS TRIUMPHANT

- Ask the children in groups to select part of the story in which evil is triumphant and create a freeze frame representing it.

- As a class look at each other's freeze frames. Explain that when you touch one of the characters within a freeze frame that character speaks aloud their thoughts. Listen to several of these.

- Hand out large strips of paper and ask each group to create a role on the wall for one character, alternatively this could be done as a whole class with just two characters. So an evil character is drawn around, and then each child writes *inside* the body outline, key phrases, ideas or descriptions of that character and the moment in the tale. Title these life size pictures.

PLANNING TO RESCUE SITA

- Revisit the list of characters and explain you want to explore the good folk in the tale too. Remind the children how Hanuman, the Monkey-King and son of the Wind God helps the exiled princess. Tell the children you are going to take the role of Hanuman at the Council of the Bears and Monkeys when they meet to discuss whether they can rescue Sita. Ask for volunteers to take the roles of Prince Rama and Prince Lakshmana, who will be questioned about the kidnapping of Sita. Remind them that this meeting goes back in time to before Sita is rescued.

- Ask the children to decide in small groups whether they are bears or monkeys, and what ideas they might have for finding and rescuing Sita. This will act as preparation for a whole group meeting and will enable you to talk to and support the volunteers who are going to be Rama and Lakshmana at that meeting.

- Discuss with the class how to physically set up the drama space for the Council meeting, and then rearrange the space appropriately.

- Begin the meeting in the role of Hanuman, and call the Council of the animals to order, asking the venerable bears and your friends, the monkeys, to take their seats. Invite the two Princes, Rama and Lakshmana, to explain their predicament and then open the meeting to the floor. Are there questions anyone wishes to ask? What suggestions can they offer? Prompts for discussion could include: who else could be trusted to help – how can demons be defeated – Sita will be guarded, how can they rescue her? This should not be a re-enactment but a general re-embodiment which stresses the dangers involved for the animals, and shows the altruistic role that Hanuman played. It is important for the teacher in role to question each speaker in order to deepen what is already known, and help details to be established, reinforcing the attitudes and behaviour associated with helping others.

GOOD TRIUMPHS OVER EVIL

- Ask the children to select part of the story in which good is triumphant over evil and create a group freeze frame of that section.

- Together observe each freeze frame, and again as teacher touch various characters who speak aloud their thoughts.

- Hand out large strips of paper to create another role on the wall. Use another colour for outlines of these good characters. Again, let the children write *inside* the characters' outlines, descriptions, key words and phrases about the nature of the characters. Title these life size pictures.

Resolutions: Drawing the Drama Together

DECIDING ON OUR OWN VIEWS

- Spread all the role on the wall sheets (both good and evil) over the floor. Encourage the children to walk around the room and read the phrases written in the character outlines. Ask the children to consider the characters portrayed, what are their views of them? Try to establish a quiet reflective time to undertake this.

- Suggest the children select a character from those depicted and write their views about this character *outside* its body outline.

- Discuss their responses to the various character traits demonstrated, together as a class. Can they suggest parallels from fiction, in which the characters are altruistic, good or evil?

- Extend this discussion to include the meaning of the faith tale and the moral issues it raises.

> You think you'd be bored?
> — Teacher

> I think it would be pretty boring, you don't get much stuff to do on the island. Well you get work but not anything nice to do.
> — Liam

> Not nice at all, because like you said they kept on telling lies, so they might be telling tales on you.
> — Sarah

> People who tell lies can't be trusted.
> — Matthew

> Yeah, it would be sad, because you couldn't trust anyone and you'd be bossed about by Ravana. It would be horrible to be **his** slave.
> — Jade

> If you weren't allowed ever to be nice, well everyone would pick on one another, it'd be dreadful.
> — Sarah

(8 year olds)

Extension Activities

- Create lists of goodies and baddies, heroes, heroines and villains in faith tales, traditional tales and other literature. Create a display of pictures of these folk from illustrated texts.

- Read a more extensive version of the tale to the class and link the tale to Divali, the Festival of Light. Madhur Jaffrey's *Seasons of Splendour: Tales, Myths and Legends of India,* (1985, Penguin), offers strong tales such as 'Magic Herb Mountain' and 'Sita in the Fire'. The high quality illustrations by Michael Foreman could be used to prompt further character discussions.

- Cut out, or recall, from newspapers and/or TV, examples of altruistic behaviour shown by members of society, or create a display of books in which characters help one another in their hour of need.

> I know who was the cleverest and the kindest, it was that monkey 'cos he knew what he wanted to do and he could've been hurt, and it wasn't even his wife, it was a human, not even an animal.
>
> Simone (aged 7)

Resourcing Further Drama from Faith Tales

Many faith tales contain strong images of the people involved, as well as the powerful predicaments they face, so these offer clear support for classroom drama. Drama enables us to sensitively explore concepts in religious education such as good and evil, the uniqueness of individuals, the awe and wonder imbued by nature and a sense of the spiritual. It can provoke questions and discussions about many issues which children find puzzling. Through the process of engagement in role their understanding can be developed.

In exploring traditional faith tales through drama, the children's understanding of a particular religion and the significant people within it, can be enriched, as well as their awareness of social and moral issues. Different versions of these tales are available, but if concerns exist with regard to representing the tale 'accurately', then we recommend reading your chosen version aloud to the class before using dramatic action to investigate it and explore the themes within it.

Extracts from the source can also be read aloud during the drama, and modern day parallels made in relation to the behaviour of the characters, as well as contemporary social expectations considered. We recommend the following faith tale collections and picture book retellings from different perspectives.

Elizabeth Brevitty and Sandra Palmer (1993) *A Tapestry of Tales*, Educational Collins.
Margaret Mayo and Louise Brierley (1995) *The Orchard Book of Creation Stories*, Orchard Books.
Nick Butterworth and Mike Inkpen (1994) *The House on the Rock*, Collins Picture Lions.
Nick Butterworth and Mike Inkpen (1994) *The Rich Farmer*, Collins Picture Lions.
Nick Butterworth and Mike Inkpen (1994) *The Good Stranger*, Collins Picture Lions.
Nick Butterworth and Mike Inkpen (1994) *The Ten Silver Coins*, Collins Picture Lions.
John Ryan (1998) *The Very Hungry Lions*, Lion.
Sarah Hayes and Inga Moore (1992) *Away in a Manager*, Walker.

Chapter 12

AN OBJECT: TOYS IN THE BIG BEDROOM

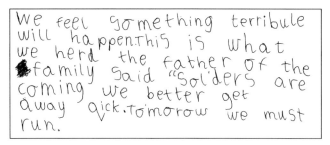

We feel something terrible will happen. This is what we herd the father of the family said "Soliders are coming we better get away qick. Tomorow we must run.

Ravi (aged 7)

Introduction

The use of an object as a drama resource is no different in principle from other starting points. In this drama a teddy bear is used, because it is rich in emotional meaning and is often an intimate and favourite toy. This drama is more appropriate for older KS1/early KS2 children because they will probably have more awareness of the kinds of real events which it addresses.

The teddy bear and other toys come from the big bedroom of two young children who are forced to leave their home with their parents, as a result of some vaguely defined civil war and great unrest in their country. Where this place is can remain unknown in the drama, but it was initially undertaken whilst the Kosovan crisis was a daily reality in the media and was deliberately taught as an analogy for some of the issues which the people of Kosovo had to face. Initially it was not related specifically to Kosovo, it was the children who made that connection as the drama unfolded. The big bedroom is the central setting of the drama, and the children are in role as the toys which have been left behind by the fleeing family. From here, they observe a number of people, hear about events in the war and perceive the effects it has upon those caught up in it. The children also take up roles as refugees at the close of the drama.

The drama convention highlighted is **teacher in role**, which is indispensable here, for the teacher brings different roles into the situation which represent the issues for examination. **Narration** is also needed to provide continuity between episodes, to heighten tension and make sense of the larger unfolding picture outside the big bedroom.

Avoiding the children's suggestions and responses in order to follow the plan may mean that real opportunities for relevant learning are missed. A professional balance between teaching objectives and children's interests is always required.

Teaching Objectives and Learning Areas
- Explore the plight of refugees (*the content of the drama*)
- Develop a language of feeling and concern (*language*)
- Develop empathy through increased understanding (*the imagination*).

Prior Experience and Materials
- No additional experience is required, since having toys in their own bedroom will provide a reassuring sense of place and familiarity with the scenario.
- The teacher's teddy.
- A drum.

First Encounters: Creating the Drama Context

THE BIG BEDROOM

- Show the class your teddy and talk a little about its importance. Invite the children to talk about their favourite toys and where they are kept.

- Ask the children to make individual statues of toys of varying status, such as their favourite, one that was thrown away, the broken or the lost one, the one placed high up, the one which listens, happy or sad toys.

- During these different representations go up to children and ask them to tell you about what they are showing. While you are doing this, intersperse it with a running commentary, as if you were moving about a bedroom with all the toys in it. This will help them to build up a mental picture of a room, which will become the big bedroom of the drama.

- Turn this narration at its conclusion into setting the scene of the drama by introducing two named children, e.g. Daniela and Mattias, and their parents. Suggest that this bedroom is special, because the toys in it come to life when no-one is present. Add tension by narrating that one evening the toys sensed trouble afoot, they heard anxious and agitated voices downstairs.

- Ask the children to work in pairs to decide what was the cause of the fear in the people's voices. Listen as a class to the possibilities, and let the children respond to one another's suggestions.

- Pass out paper and let the children write in role as one of the toys. Who are they? What is happening?

> My name is Ted. I live on a little boys bed. He dos not no that I come to life in the dark. I can see evrething and I can here evrething. There was lots of shouting outdoors. there were bangs and screems. we all sat on the bed close to the big bunny. Mattias was crying, he said he didn't want to leeve. Then he pickt me up and put me in his ruksak. It's dark in here. . . .

Jake (aged 8)

Conflicts and Resolutions: Developing the Drama

THE REFUGEES FLEE

- In role as a parent, call your family (the class) together, and tell them of the mounting persecution and civil war, which others, like yourselves, are experiencing. Explain that after a difficult discussion with your husband/wife, you've decided the family must leave tonight, while it is still safe, so the children must all pack their important possessions and prepare to leave. This narration needs to call upon the real dangers and recollect the images, which are all too common in such situations, in order to help the children imagine some of the feelings which might come from this kind of experience.

- In role as a parent, tell them that they can take only one toy with them. In prompting them to look through their toys and choose one, ask your children which they've chosen and why.
- Ask the children in small groups to construct two freeze frames, one of the family leaving the home and the other at some point during their escape. In watching some of these, link the two freeze frames with rapid drum beats to enable the group to re-form.

The Big Bedroom

Hello, I'm a little polly pocket called polly. I'm tiny and I have loads of freinds and I'm happy in my life. The bedroom I live in a navey curtains, it is Danielas room. Last night I was chatting with a doll when we heard mother say we have to leave, you can only bring one toy. The Soldiers are coming to envade our contry. In a few minutes we set off down the lane then suddenly the car broke down. oh no I said to myself and we had to wait and wait and wait. But suddenly there came a noise, it was soldiers, they said "Get out of your car and walk" so we got out. We didn't know where to go.

Abigail (aged 8)

AN INTRUDER ARRIVES

- Switch the scenario back to the big bedroom and ask the children to take up the positions of the remaining toys left behind in that bedroom. Describe in some detail, the turmoil and the untidy state the fleeing family had to leave the house in. Additionally, include a description of the sounds and images of the in-coming 'army' of occupation breaking into the unoccupied houses and searching for loot.
- Narrate and mime the noisy entry into the house of a soldier (you in role) and his brief and random search of the bedroom. Watched by the toys search around and snatch what you want before being called away by the shouts of your fellow soldiers.
- Suggest the toys whisper to one another about what has been happening.

A SAFE HOME

- Interrupt this by narrating the entry of other people. The toys hear a number of softer footsteps coming up the stairs, the door opens and into the bedroom come what looks like a family or group of exhausted and scared refugees, who are trying to find a safe retreat from the soldiers. Once again include as many details as possible from the media images of such unfortunate people.
- Ask the children to create a freeze frame of that family at that moment in small groups.
- Ask a few figures in the freeze frame their thoughts and feelings, and then extend this by narrating the brief details of their stay in the room, and their hasty departure next morning.
- Explain that as they go one of the children picks up a toy, and asks if they can take it. Discuss with the children what an adult might reply, in order to raise issues about ownership and the pressures of exceptional circumstances.

CAN YOU HELP ME?

- Ask the class to take up their toy positions again and watch carefully as the last individual arrives. Describe the person's frightened and bedraggled demeanour, and in role, mime their cautious entry into the room. This refugee will be you in role. In your mind hold to the knowledge that you knew the original owners of the house and that you are coming to their house in the hope of refuge and help. Call out their names, Daniela, Mattias, Oliver and talk or mutter to yourself about them, giving the watching children more understanding of your identity. You will need to portray this person at the point of exhaustion and desperation. Conclude your portrayal by slumping into a chair, and narrate the person going to sleep, to dream about what has been happening in their troubled country.

- Stand up and step out of role, suggesting that in the next activity you want the toys individually to come up to the exhausted sleeping fugitive and whisper in their ear some words of advice, help or support.

- Help this to happen, by sitting in the chair and 'going to sleep', bow your head so you're not looking at the children. Arrange with one confident child that they will begin when they judge that the fugitive is asleep.

- During your 'sleep', move fitfully but not to the point of being disturbing, and let the children choose to come up to you. Be patient and allow the silence of your role to increase the tension and move the children. Only if necessary, pause and come out of role, to prompt more of them to try whispering advice.

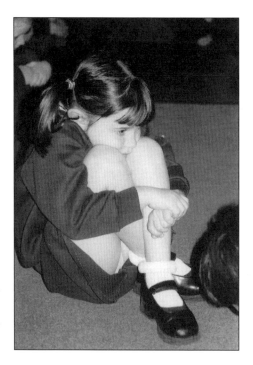

Resolutions: Drawing the Drama Together

A HALF – WAY HOME

- Narrate the formation of a tented refugee camp and the arrival of Daniela and Mattias's family who are obliged to set up home there. In groups ask them to list all the things that they think the family would need, or be able to find, to live in these conditions.

- In role as an UNHCR official, call the refugees together. Tell them that they're unable to return to their homes at present because of the uncertainty of the situation, and then ask for information about them as refugees. Listen to their stories of leaving home and their journeys and ask them to identify all the sick and needy people in their group. Discuss appropriate priorities for treating sick people at the small field hospital.

- Create a whole class freeze frame of the hospital and the refugee camp through individual, pair or group portrayals.

- In role as a news reporter, move amongst them asking questions to find out about the refugees' needs. What should you tell the world about their plight? How could other nations help? You might compose some headlines together about the situation or even write short news articles.

- Out of role, discuss with the children their feelings and reactions to the drama, and make links with similar events e.g. East Timor, Kosovo, Chechnaya, endeavouring to develop their awareness of such situations and their empathy with refugees.

Extension Activities

- As a class write to relevant charities e.g. Oxfam, Red Cross, for information about such situations and consider how the class might help.

- Conjecture what might happen to the people in the drama in the future and maybe turn this into a class written story, or improvise possible events.

- Each child could create a time-line for a refugee child in the camp, reflecting life events before and after their flight to safety.

- Ask the children as toys to make a drawing of what they saw at an important point in the story.

Resourcing Further Drama from Objects

Objects are useful resources; their tangibility helps children believe in the ideas generated from them. The actual presence of the object seems to proffer a sense of reality which draws children into the drama, but leaves plenty of questions unanswered, e.g. who owns/owned the object, what they used it for and what it represents can all become issues for examination. Examples include the following different types of objects.

1   The Old

A Victorian washboard could be shown and its use in the past explored through a drama focusing on contrasting lifestyles. An old wood plane might be used to contextualise a drama around the building of wooden sailing ships and the Voyages of Discovery. An ancient key could be used to open hidden doors, treasure chests, attic boxes or magic cupboards. Any world can be visited by using an ancient key to offer entry into alternative universes.

2   The Exotic

A large costume ring or brooch could evoke the magical world of Kings/Queens or Fairies/Goblins in which the struggle of good and evil is played out. A broken statue/china object could be used to prompt an exploration

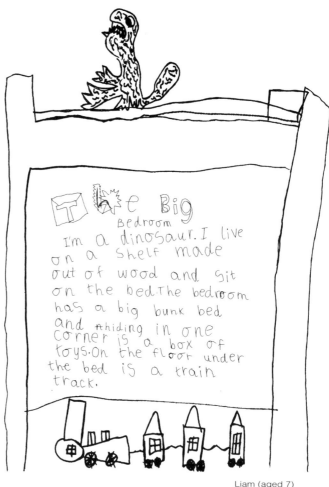

The Big Bedroom
I'm a dinosaur. I live on a shelf made out of wood and sit on the bed. The bedroom has a big bunk bed and hiding in one corner is a box of toys. On the floor under the bed is a train track.

Liam (aged 7)

of how and why it was chipped. Who did this, what were the consequences? Examining the rich clothing of a Maharajah's daughter, and perhaps by contrast her maidservant's clothes, could prompt a drama set in India about power and authority.

3   The Everyday

A personal possession such as a handbag or wallet could be found and lead to suppositions about its owner, their life, past and present. A note or half finished letter or code which gives partial information about a situation could also create a mystery to be solved. Alternatively, an apparently ordinary pair of glasses could prompt discussion about whose they are and what special properties they possess. These too could provide a form of transport into another world or prompt an investigation into their owner's life.

**teaching
in
role**

talking
and
writing

Chapter 13

PLANNING CLASSROOM DRAMA

Introduction

Classroom drama is more often than not focused upon people and relies upon their life stories, which can be fact or fiction, or a combination of both. In drama we make-believe we are other people in other places, living in other times, but facing ordinary but significant human problems. So planning a single lesson or a series of drama lessons, involves a process of identifying a general area of interest (often a curriculum context), and the key features of a related human narrative: the people, the place they are in, and the predicament they face. The specific areas of learning and teaching objectives also need to be identified.

A wealth of resources are available which offer the teacher a partial basis on which to build. The re-enactment of any text is best avoided, but each text, artefact, curriculum focus or tale can be usefully employed to support planning. If you explore the gaps in a text, or seek to examine the history of an artefact, or co-author a new tale, then the drama can remain open-ended and can harness the children's imaginations whilst still responding to the identified areas of learning.

When the general focus, the narrative elements and the specific learning areas have been identified, then an actual session can be mapped out. The map will include a series of dramatic activities which enable the children to step into the imaginary world, focus upon certain tensions and conflicts in it and seek to resolve these and reflect upon them. So each drama session can usefully be divided into three major sections.

- *First Encounters: Creating the Drama Context.* This involves introducing and establishing the narrative elements of people, place and predicament.
- *Conflicts and Tensions: Developing the Drama.* This involves focusing upon and investigating the major dramatic tension and learning areas.
- *Resolutions: Drawing the Drama Together.* This involves harnessing the children's ideas and insights, shaping the culmination to the fiction, and reflecting upon their learning.

Follow up work or extension activities outside the dramatic context, may also be planned to summarise or extend the children's learning. The actual map of the drama session offers you, the teacher, considerable structural security and should allow you to feel safe since you will have anticipated some of the likely responses to the tensions. However, teaching is not a science or a manufacturing process. You will need to keep an open and flexible attitude towards your plan, and exercise your professional judgement about when to follow it and when to re-organise it in the light of the children's responses during the drama. If the plan is adhered to during the first session, the following session could build upon the classes expressed interests or be planned in response to your assessment of their learning. Occasionally, you may completely refocus the session, allowing the children to lead the drama in an unexpected direction. Overall, however, you retain considerable responsibility for what takes place and must seek both to guide the children towards particular activities and teaching/learning objectives as well as to respond to their questions and interests by integrating these into your sessions.

A   A General Area of Focus

The drama will be linked to a general learning area within the curriculum, so the planning process will often begin with a current topic or theme. For example, if you are focussing on famous people from the past this might prompt you into planning a drama about Grace Darling or if you are focussing on traditional tales this might prompt a trip through the magic mirror to the world of Coyote or Ananse.

The Planning Process

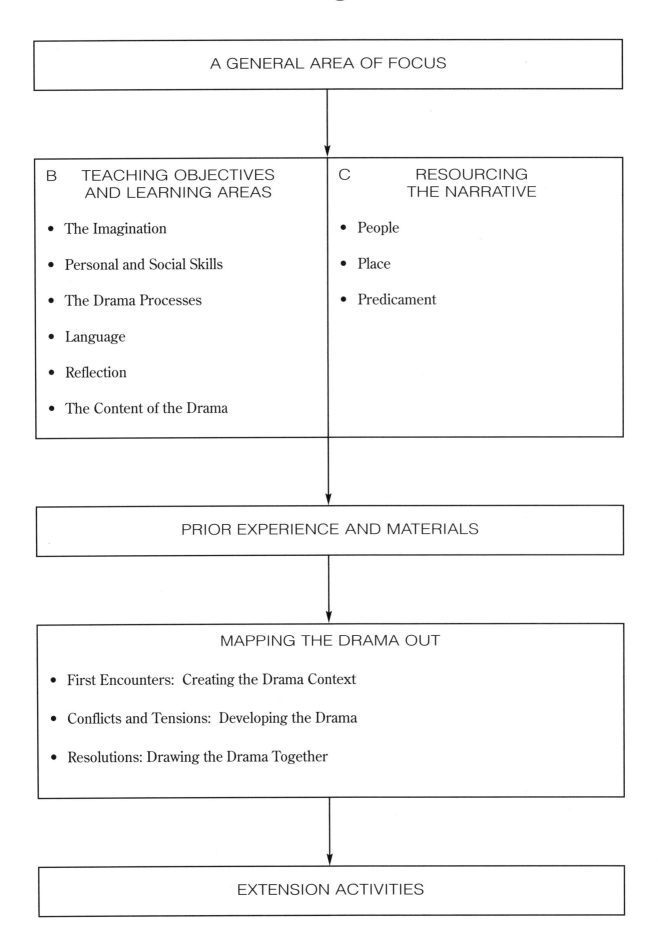

A GENERAL AREA OF FOCUS

B TEACHING OBJECTIVES
   AND LEARNING AREAS

- The Imagination

- Personal and Social Skills

- The Drama Processes

- Language

- Reflection

- The Content of the Drama

C RESOURCING
   THE NARRATIVE

- People

- Place

- Predicament

PRIOR EXPERIENCE AND MATERIALS

MAPPING THE DRAMA OUT

- First Encounters: Creating the Drama Context

- Conflicts and Tensions: Developing the Drama

- Resolutions: Drawing the Drama Together

EXTENSION ACTIVITIES

B   Teaching Objectives and Learning Areas

Explicit teaching objectives encourage the teacher to keep the session focused. The teaching objectives need to be identified and carefully integrated into the plan when mapping out the session. This will ensure that the children's attainment in these areas is visible and that the teacher can judge the extent to which learning has taken place and which particular areas need further development.

The source of the teaching objectives are the six areas of learning in drama. These all interrelate and are dependent upon one another; for instance, empathy is an act of the imagination, as well as part of a developing personal outlook. They are separated for the purpose of planning and assessment, Chapter 14 provides an elaboration of these. The learning areas include:

- the imagination
- personal and social skills
- the drama processes
- language
- reflection
- the content of the drama.

Practically it is only possible to select two or three learning areas and related teaching objectives to focus upon in any given drama session, in response to the children's needs, the narrative elements and the general area of focus. Over time, the tailored teaching objectives need to reflect all six areas of learning in drama. For example, in planning a lesson around Grace Darling, the teacher, knowing her life history, may decide to work upon empathy and develop the children's knowledge of this heroine, as well as their ability to use language appropriately, according to audience and purpose. So the specific teaching objectives and learning areas of this drama might include the following, (the learning areas are in italics):

- show empathy and sensitivity to others (*personal and social skills*)
- know more about Grace's role in the Forfarshayr shipwreck (*the content of the drama*)
- use different spoken registers (*language*).

Alongside the tailored teaching objectives, many other learning opportunities exist because of the embracing nature of drama. Teachers need to seek a balance in relation to the planned objectives and the unplanned learning opportunities that may emerge. Experience certainly shows that to ignore the children's interest all the time, risks turning drama into an entirely teacher directed activity, and losing the children's creativity and commitment. It also fails to develop their independence in drama.

C   Resourcing the Narrative:
People, Place and Predicament

The three elements of narrative: 'people, place and predicament' are the basic components around which individual drama sessions can be mapped. As the planning diagram indicates, these are chosen alongside the learning areas, but must be selected before the dramatic action can be mapped out. *A variety of resources* can be used to help plan the people, place and predicament in the drama. Teachers do not need to create these narrative elements themselves, but can turn to short story collections, picture books, traditional tales, folk and fairy tales, myths, legends and faith tales, all of which contain these elements. However, published tales do not represent the only resource. Visuals of all kinds: paintings and sculpture, photographs and comic strips, TV extracts and artefacts, as well as illustrations from picture books and individual poems all offer starting points. For example, a painting of a child might prompt the teacher to consider the character who is portrayed (e.g. who is she, what's she feeling, why does she look uncertain) and then decide upon a place for the drama (e.g. a pier) and a predicament (e.g. she becomes separated from her parents). Drama can also be resourced by selecting one or more of the narrative elements from visual, musical or poetic resources and then inventing the remaining elements in response to these.

The life stories of historically significant people also lend themselves to the planning process, although only one aspect of their life is needed for a drama. This will not involve historical re-enactment but may focus, for example, on an in-depth examination of the many challenges which beset Florence Nightingale and the personal resources she found to cope with them. In addition, scientific and geographical themes can be used as a source base. For example, in a drama on nutrition, the place could be a new health food café, the people, employees of the café, and the predicament mice have been found and the hygiene inspector is due!

In using various resources to establish the people, place and predicament of the drama, you may also wish to integrate the resource into the actual drama. For example, by reading an extract from the chosen poem during the drama or by showing the photograph or artefact to the class. Depending on the maturity and experience of the class, you can actually involve them in the planning process, so that their ideas contribute to the initial mapping out of the narrative elements.

1   PEOPLE

The roles children are given, or adopt, have a marked influence on their possible learning. Children need to know who they are before they can react with ease and authenticity in drama, so their initial forays into role will be more successful if the roles selected are fairly close to their own experience. For example in Hey Diddle Diddle (Ch.1), the children play themselves on an exciting adventure into The Topsy Turvy World. In other drama, the class may still be in role as children but in another place and time, as in Bimwili and the Zimwi (Ch.5), when they take up the roles of Bimwili's siblings. By contrast, in The Butterfly Farm (Ch.10) the children are given the mantle of expertise, and remain in role throughout as entomologists.

In selecting various roles for the children, you'll need to identify the kind of characters likely to be found in a particular place and take into account the children's age and experience. You might be in a position to challenge the children to adopt several roles. Switching from one role to another during the drama, as in The New Park (Ch.7) offers potentially richer learning. But switching imaginative perspectives can be confusing and may result in affirming superficial stereotypes if not handled carefully.

Roles are developed in the imaginary context, e.g. through working as sailors and scrubbing the decks, hoisting the sail, cooking in the galley and responding to predicaments. The historical time frame of the drama will also influence the roles adopted, in which case it may be that the children will benefit from undertaking some background research prior to the drama, but they will need to make the roles their own. You may need to extend some licence for interpretation of the facts by the children, which you can re-address during your reflection time, if you consider the accepted historical line has been grossly disturbed.

The role adopted is the perspective from which children learn, so you'll need to select characters whose predicaments and experiences will enable the learning areas to be examined. By working in different roles with the class, you can extend the role repertoire available to the children, through offering them the opportunity to take up a range of roles associated with your role, as well as challenging the children to think inside the roles. So the teacher's roles also need to be identified at the planning stage.

2 PLACE

Drama has to happen somewhere, and since it is only through the imagination that drama takes place at all, it is clear that visualising/creating the place in which the drama is going to take place is an important initial activity. The place or setting will also influence the kind of characters who could inhabit the story, and the conflicts and tensions which might arise. It is not that the children become the forest and the trees, but that in exploring the forest together they can build their sense of this imaginary place. For example, in Hey Diddle Diddle (Ch.1) the children explore a Topsy Turvy World in which normal expectations are overturned, before they discover an upside down house. In selecting the place in which the drama operates, the teacher needs to find a suitable venue which will enable the learning areas to be developed. In addition, a balance needs to be established between:

- *Real world examples* – such as a park, a rubbish dump, a club-house or a school
- *Fantasy examples* – such as The Land of Nursery Rhymes, The Land at the End of the Rainbow, The Kingdom under the Sea or The Castle in the Clouds
- *Book based examples* – such as the land from Where the Wild Things Are, One Eyed Jack the Pirate Chief's ship, or Baba Yaga's home of bones.

The role play area can usefully be related to the venue for classroom drama, promoting further investigations. This works particularly well when the place for the unfolding classroom drama remains constant for several weeks. Then work in one context feeds work in the other.

3 PREDICAMENT

Without experiencing a genuine sense of conflict or tension, through their engagement in role as characters in the situations they encounter, there would be no drama. The children may initially be interested in the people and keen to build a sense of place, but it is through their response to the predicament that their commitment deepens and they experience the drama as real.

Dramatic conflicts or tensions trigger the 'electricity' of drama, because they involve some element of anticipation, a sense of waiting or uncertainty in relation to some unresolved situation. A variety of tensions and predicaments exist in life and therefore fiction and you'll need to select one which suits your class and your chosen learning areas. Predicaments may relate to any of the following tensions:

- *challenges* – obstacles which need to be overcome
- *limitations* – factors which inhibit or constrain the intended direction of events
- *decisions* – the pros and cons of the situation which have to be assessed
- *destiny* – the influence of chance or fate as well as fixed social or moral expectations
- *changes* – alterations to the status quo that produce new predicaments or tensions
- *ignorance* – being unaware of significant factors which cause difficulties
- *waiting* – this often heralds change and challenge, as well as compounding stress
- *misunderstanding* – mismatches and misreading situations can bring conflict.

Predicaments in drama demand the children's involvement, and require them to respond to the situation in which they find themselves, without knowing where it will lead. The predicament forms the dynamo to drama, the personal commitment and affective involvement which enables children to learn from living and feeling inside the drama.

D   Prior Experience and Materials

Once the narrative structure of people, place, predicament has been resourced and the learning areas identified, the teacher can discern what experiences would be preferable for the children to have undertaken prior to the drama. In many cases, no specific previous experience will be necessary in others if you are integrating the drama into an area of the curriculum, you'll need to carefully consider where to place the drama sessions in your medium term plan. Any materials needed can be noted in the plan.

E   Mapping Out the Drama Session

Using the ideas for people, place and predicament, the teacher can map out an extended sequence of activities which constitute the drama session. A range of drama conventions will be employed to investigate the issues and respond to the teaching objectives and learning areas identified. Each session can be divided into three sections; first encounters, conflicts and tensions and finally resolutions.

1. FIRST ENCOUNTERS: CREATING THE DRAMA CONTEXT

This phase of your drama establishes two essentials. Firstly, it needs to 'hook' the children's interest, which is the responsive side of their imaginations and the basic motivation for their involvement and subsequent learning. Secondly, it needs to establish the world in which the drama takes place, through the people, place and predicament elements. The predicament is the primary initiator of the drama, as it is the children's response to this which creates their thoughts and actions in the drama.

Your initial drama strategy needs to open intriguing 'doors' for the class, to generate involvement and capture their imaginations. Lengthy class discussions need to be avoided at this juncture, rather the children's ideas need to be encouraged through *early imaginative activity*. The resource chapters utilise a wide range of strategies to spark interest and establish a framework on which the drama can build. The resource itself may provide an initial prompt, for example the poem in Through That Door (Ch.3) or part of a story may be told as in The Bakerloo Flea (Ch.9). These begin to offer information about imaginative contexts to which the children can respond. There are many other ways to step into the world of drama which work well with young children, since they appeal to their sense of adventure and prompt their imagination to produce ideas and actions, as well as visual images.

Many drama teachers argue that the most powerful way of engaging children is by using the medium itself, through the *teacher in role* presenting the predicament to the children, as in The King who was Afraid (Ch.6). Real people, particularly when they are 'unknown' to the children, generate an initial and compelling interest. Their three dimensional nature seems to demand attention, and if you manipulate your role, you can present the predicament which you embody so the children take it on themselves. Also, because you are involved in the drama, the children will follow you into the situation, you are the model for their participation. In other words, if you do it they'll do it! In addition, you're able to address their tentative questions and comments from within the drama, which helps them to orientate themselves in the situation and begin to make sense of it. The longer you sustain the role with their full attention, the more deeply they'll become involved. Another strategy is to use narration, and become the storyteller. You can create atmosphere and tension, help the children create visual images, and pass on information, which builds the context and background about the people and the impending predicament.

Various kinds of 'magic' are also useful as initial strategies which facilitate *imaginative access to other worlds*. Magic carpets or time machines can take you and your class anywhere, back in time, into the future, across oceans, up into space. This kind of strategy appeals to younger children, and it begins to exercise part of their imagination. Real objects can become magic, so a key opens doors into other lands, or a small box filled with something which rattles can become magic powder, which when sprinkled upon the children, carries them off to another place. Magic windows or mirrors can also enable travel. Similarly, creating special chants or spells, rhymes or wishes can add an extra component to the start of a drama. The class can write their own oral chant incorporating rhythm and repetition, action and movement. Such a drama chant with very young children, mobilises their imaginations and can help them step into the drama, for their words become actions, taking them into another world. Creating and making a corporate map of the place to which they will travel, or have travelled, can also help children visualise the place.

These first encounters need to help young children establish a strong sense of the place and themselves as people, so that when they encounter predicaments they can respond quickly and become committed to resolving the conflict. Their imaginations need to be triggered into action through early mental engagement in the fictional world.

2. CONFLICTS AND TENSIONS: DEVELOPING THE DRAMA

As the drama with its incidents unfolds, the dramatic tension increasingly holds the children's attention, and opens up the themes, which will be used to explore the learning areas. During this time the class become more involved in the issues beneath the narrative they are creating. At first their imaginary world may be somewhat superficial and oriented towards enthusiastic dramatic action, but with your guidance and through your selection of appropriate drama conventions, their work will grow in depth and insight. Later, through creating and reflecting upon this imaginary world, the children come to understand themselves and the real world in which they live, because the drama world is an analogy for the real world.

The range of drama conventions and symbols planned in this section will need to keep the drama moving and ensure variety and pace, as well as provide the opportunity to investigate the learning areas. Since each convention provides particular kinds of support and shapes the drama in various ways, the children's involvement can be deepened through the use of appropriate techniques, which offer new perspectives, open up dilemmas, and examine moral choices, as well as their consequences. Once again we recommend the convention of teacher in role for its flexibility and power.

Once the class has begun to examine the issues in the narrative, their developing views and insights may prompt questions or identify *areas of interest* which don't coincide with their teacher's plans. Initially, it may be preferable to pursue the activities you've planned, and merely log the children's particular interests in order to explore them in a future session. With experience however, you'll find you can respond to some of the children's interests and re-orient the session whilst still bearing in mind the intended teaching objectives/learning areas.

In this phase of the drama, when the conflicts and tensions come to the fore, the class will move constantly between being active and being thoughtful. They will live in the drama (e.g. whisper into Ravana's ear), as well as being more detached (e.g. discuss why the King keeps his daughter a virtual prisoner). These *moves between engagement and reflection* are not overtly marked, but are an integral part of your developing drama and need to be mapped into the plan. They are also mental preparations for the deeper reflection that makes up the concluding phase.

3. RESOLUTIONS: DRAWING THE DRAMA TOGETHER

In this part of the drama, the children continue to work together through action and reflection to resolve the drama predicament, reach a reasonable conclusion and then think about their drama. In mapping this out, the teacher can focus more explicitly upon the teaching objectives/learning areas and issues to be examined as the fictional world closes. Once a resolution has been established, techniques which help children *express the insights gained* through the drama can be employed. This may well involve discussion, drawing or shared writing to summarise the views, positions, themes and morals examined. *Making connections* will be a central focus at this time, whether these are personal parallels, connections to particular characters or themes in other stories or connections in relation to school, home, community or the wider world. The diversity of insights gained need to be articulated, shared and valued.

This phase of the drama should offer the children the space and time to digest the dramatic experience and *revisit some of the teaching objectives and learning areas.* The teacher may focus on different learning areas over time, so that, for example, on some occasions the curriculum content will be profiled, on others, the drama process itself and the conventions used, will be discussed or the personal and social issues will be foregrounded in this drawing together time. This provides the teacher with the opportunity to offer explicit feedback to the class and to assess their understanding at the close of the drama.

F   Extension Activities

As the drama draws to a close, you need to gauge the appropriateness of various pre-planned extension activities, based partly on an assessment of the children's learning. Activities across the whole breadth of the primary curriculum can be undertaken, although tenuous links need to be avoided and those activities which respond to the children's expressed interests during the drama, and which continue to pursue the learning areas should take preference. Such work has the potential to build on the insights gained, revisit the issues examined and give voice to the responses generated. The class could be invited to join the teacher in generating their own list of possible activities. These might include retelling sections of the tale on tape, creating storyboards, writing playscripts or scenes, making posters to advertise a film version, producing newspaper articles, writing in role as one of the characters or co-authoring a class book. However, there may be no need to extend the drama; in fact the class may benefit most from leaving the work to be imaginatively revisited in the playground or role play area.

A PLANNING CHECKLIST

Having identified the teaching objectives/learning areas, resourced the narrative elements and created a map of your session, including first encounters, conflicts and tensions and resolutions, you'd be well advised to read through your plan. A number of points are worth considering. These include:

1.   What is the early narrative hook to invite the learners into the imaginative world?

2.   Are a variety of drama conventions employed to investigate the issue?

3.   Does the sequence of activities provide a varied pace and rhythm, so there are moments of relative stillness and focused reflection, as well as times of more active energetic engagement?

4.   Are the teaching objectives/learning areas woven into the fabric of the lesson? Can they be evidenced in action and reflection through the spoken and written word, in particular in the resolutions section?

5.   Is there a reasonable balance between pair, small group, and whole class work?

6.   Are the range of roles and activities the children are being invited to undertake, suitable for their age, experience and ability?

7.   Are there any children for whom the themes, issues or objectives may be very challenging? What can be planned to help them?

Chapter 14
ASSESSING CLASSROOM DRAMA

Introduction

The National Curriculum requirements for drama focus upon the three strands of arts education: making, performing and responding. These are useful and prompt a breadth of drama activities, but do not constitute sufficiently focused areas for assessing children's learning in drama. In the National Curriculum, drama is placed within English in the Programme of Study for Speaking and Listening, but to limit ourselves to merely assessing this aspect of drama would be to ignore its contribution to other areas of learning. Classroom drama involves developing six areas of learning simultaneously.

> - The Imagination
> - Personal and Social Skills
> - The Drama Processes
> - Language
> - Reflection
> - The Content of the Drama

These areas interrelate, are dependent upon one another and shift in significance at different moments in a drama. As children make, perform and respond in classroom drama, there are many opportunities for developing their learning in all of these areas. The development of each is related to children's growing independence and ability to work in depth, examining increasingly complex issues and taking more control of conventions to achieve their desired ends. These areas build upon the related *Early Learning Goals* (1999) and tie in to the wider National Curriculum requirements.

The Imagination

Classroom drama primarily relies upon the imagination, and it provides a rich opportunity for its development, through refining and enhancing established ideas as well as producing new and original ones. Progression in imaginative development in drama will involve children in:

- Recognising that drama is an activity using the imagination
- Entering imaginary situations
- Contributing ideas to develop the fictional situation, firstly as themselves and then in role
- Offering ideas originating from personal feelings, values, experience or knowledge
- Developing increasingly effective, original, clear and vivid ideas
- Consciously generating ideas to develop the drama.

Personal and Social Skills

Classroom drama allows children to develop their personal and social skills in secure imaginary contexts. These skills form the basis of their moral development. Progression in personal and social skills in drama will involve children in:

- Engaging with belief and feeling in the drama
- Increasingly identifying their own and others' particular feelings and needs in the drama
- Joining in and responding to others in small group/class work
- Developing flexibility, an ability to negotiate with others and an awareness of the consequences of their words and actions
- Developing an increasing confidence and independence in drama
- Considering with increasing depth, the moral and social issues in the drama.

The Drama Processes

Classroom drama enables children to use and understand a range of drama conventions which allow them to explore meaning and express their ideas. Progression in using the drama processes will involve children in:

- Participating in some drama conventions
- Engaging fully in a variety of drama conventions
- Recognising and using conventions with increasing independence
- Suggesting and employing conventions in order to achieve their desired effects
- Manipulating conventions with increasing ingenuity, imagination and understanding of the art form.

Language

Classroom drama fosters a wide range of spoken and written language registers, through the variety of roles adopted. It also encourages a more indepth examination of text, since drama is inference in action. Progression in language development in drama will involve children in:

- Contributing orally in imagined contexts
- Listening, responding and writing in role
- Using an increasingly wide range of spoken and written language registers
- Selecting appropriate and effective language in role according to purpose, context and audience.

Reflection

In classroom drama, children both live within a fictional context to make meanings, and step outside of it to reflect upon the unfolding drama. They also make connections between the real world and the imaginary one. Through this process children develop their reflective capacity and ability to evaluate their drama. Progression in reflective development in drama will involve children in:

- Recalling moments in the drama
- Considering and commenting upon their own and others' drama
- Critically evaluating the drama, its content and process
- Developing a capacity to view situations from differing perspectives
- Making connections between the drama and the real world
- Developing an increasing ability to identify and understand parallel situations in the real world.

The Content of the Drama

The content of each classroom drama is related to an area of the curriculum and enables the children to develop, use and refine their knowledge in this area. In developing their abilities to handle the content, children will be involved in:

- Showing awareness of the content of the drama
- Contributing to and exploring their knowledge of the content
- Developing their knowledge and understanding of the content gained from different perspectives.

How to Assess Classroom Drama

Assessment in classroom drama is the same as effective assessment elsewhere, it is formative and aids development, it is not just to record activity and progress. Through evaluating the children's engagement, as well assessing individual children's learning, you will be able to identify particular objectives for the next session. Whilst all six areas of learning in drama will develop simultaneously, for planning purposes it is preferable to identify only three areas to focus upon explicitly in a given session. The specific teaching objectives will be developed from these areas (see Ch.13). Evaluating the class's learning in relation to the teaching objectives will to some extent take place during the drama but is highlighted in the resolutions section, when the teaching objectives and learning areas are foregrounded and revisited. The writing in role or other conventions used at this stage serve to prompt reflection upon the learning areas. Clear feedback is important to help the class understand the areas of learning in drama and various forms of self assessment can be included.

Evidence of children's learning in drama can be collected through a variety of means. These include:

- observation notes made by the teacher *(during the drama or soon after)*
- verbatim quotes made by the teacher *(during the drama)*
- drawing in role *(during the drama)*
- writing in role *(during the drama or as part of follow up work)*
- brief audio taped extracts *(during the drama or as part of follow up work)*
- photographs *(also for display purposes)*
- extension activities *(after the drama)*
- self assessment activities *(after the drama)*

Since it is impossible to assess and record the whole classes learning in a single session, we advise choosing small groups of children to assess, ensuring whole class assessment over time. By focusing on only two or three children in each session, it is feasible to collect evidence of their learning in relation to the three learning areas identified. Notes in the form of verbatim quotes and comments on the use of their imagination, drama processes and ability to reflect may be made this term for example, whilst next term, a couple of pieces of annotated writing/drawing in role and an observation could be used as evidence of their learning in other areas. It is also worthwhile noting any drama contributions which you recognise as exceptional or significant for a particular child. Annual summative reporting may be short, but can help to reassure parents about learning in drama and offer evidence of their child's progression and development.

Evaluating the Quality of the Children's Engagement

The quality of the children's engagement can only be evaluated at the time. You know your children and will be able to judge the level of their engagement, what they are feeling, and their attitude towards their involvement. Playing, when important relationships and puzzling events are explored and relived, can be a very serious business. This kind of seriousness is frequently evident in drama: even when the outward appearance of the children's behaviour may seem to be expressing frivolity, but their eyes may be very intent upon what is happening, since it is important to them.

At times, powerful emotions such as outrage or anger may emerge and be quite clearly seen in their expressions, at other times their feelings may be quieter or cooler, and are closer to concentration and serious attention. The content of your drama will obviously have a strong bearing upon what kind of engagement your children develop. This is part of the personal and social area of learning and is directly concerned with the education of the sensibilities and feelings. Drama allows, even encourages, the arousal of feelings and enables the learner to experience and recognise these and begin to come to a personal understanding of them. In evaluating the children's involvement as well as their learning in drama, you will be assessing the quality of your session in more depth.

Chapter 15

MANAGING CLASSROOM DRAMA

Introduction

Drama is a powerful and motivating tool for learning, but many teachers lack the confidence to use it. Concerns about not being theatrical enough or the challenge of handling children in open-ended improvisational contexts hold back some practitioners. This chapter seeks to respond to teachers' perennial questions and concerns about managing classroom drama: maintaining control, establishing noise levels, deciding where to teach it, taking up a role, supporting shy children and dealing with difficult ones. It also discusses introducing drama to beginners, fitting it into a crowded curriculum, slowing the action down and handling sensitive issues.

Do I have to act?

Drama is commonly associated with acting, with the theatre and putting on a show, so some teachers fear they need to be extroverts to do it. This is not necessary: teaching classroom drama in the primary years is about developing children's understanding of the world, so neither you, nor the children need to be actors. You will have to take up different roles, but quietness and commitment are far more effective than any kind of histrionics.

Taking on teacher in role for the first time can be a little daunting, but remember not to act, just adopt the role, believe in the situation and speak seriously and with conviction from your imagined position. You already take on a multitude of different roles in life: as a sympathetic adult; an encouraging teacher; an exasperated parent and so forth. In classroom drama you'll simply be adopting other roles to help the children learn. Try to keep in role during drama time, since if you break it briefly with a knowing smile, the children will respond to you as their teacher, rather than respond to you in role. During the drama you will be moving in and out of role, so you will not be sustaining the role for a lengthy period of time unless you and the children are very experienced. The authentic commitment which the teacher in role demonstrates, provides a model for the children and prompts them to take a full part in the shared endeavour.

With a class who have only a limited experience of classroom drama, it would be advisable to prepare them for you going into role. Explain, for example, that you're going to walk towards the door and when you turn around and return, you'll be in role as the police superintendent. Initially you might select high profile or more controlling roles for yourself until you feel ready to take a more vulnerable role. All roles however offer you the chance to make suggestions, ask questions and shape the unfolding drama. If the children are surprised by your behaviour in role (because it's different from usual), they may become giggly, but by continuing to take your role seriously they will quickly respond in kind and engage in the drama alongside you. Children's interest and motivation in drama are both very high, and they appreciate, enjoy and learn from the full involvement of their teacher.

What if I don't think I have enough imagination to teach classroom drama?

Don't worry! The chapters in this book show how a variety of resources can be relied upon to prompt the classes imaginative engagement. The teacher simply joins them on this journey, sharing in the process of exploration and making use of a range of drama conventions to imaginatively investigate the issue at hand. Your imagination (which is the ability to make connections between ideas in any form) is in constant use in everyday contexts, ranging from 'what can I concoct for supper from what's in the store-cupboard', to dealing sensitively with a child in trouble. It is a capacity we all have; although some people claim not to be imaginative, what they are probably saying is that they are not 'artistic'! Be that as it may, in classroom drama, your enthusiasm, commitment, natural imaginative capacity and preparedness to be open, to consider alternatives and try are more than sufficient to make the drama successful. Any shortcomings you feel you might have, will easily be outweighed by the children's energy and willingness to have a go.

How can I maintain control?

Some teachers avoid drama because they are afraid of possible discipline problems and are concerned that the children will just 'mess about'. Quality drama demands self discipline and concentration, careful planning and the use of simple control strategies. The most essential of these is a 'stop' signal: a clap of the hands, beat of a drum/tambour, hand held high above the head, or you sitting in the teacher's chair. The children should be forewarned of the signal and the first time you introduce it, they should practice it in a game. There needs to be clear guidance too about the use of space and objects which might be to hand. We recommend that nothing is used by the children, except their imagination and perhaps occasionally, simple pieces of furniture.

Children become actively involved in drama, expressing themselves with enthusiasm, movement and energy. This is a significant characteristic of drama, and acknowledges the role the body plays in the generation of ideas, but needs to be balanced with reflective opportunities and moments of relative stillness. In planning the classroom drama session, you'll find you can harness their energy and focus their thinking by using a variety of drama conventions, (see Ch.17), which offer a balance between free movement and more static work. For example, some conventions, such as small group improvisation, offer more freedom of movement than others. The balance of the planned activities supports the teacher's control and also helps give pace and rhythm to the session.

One of the most crucial control mechanisms in drama is the teacher in role. From inside the drama, you can influence and shape the dramatic enquiry and legitimately maintain control in helping the children consider the consequences of their actions. In questioning their decisions and providing time outside the drama to consider the situation, the teacher is able to retain the reins of the drama whenever necessary. You'll gradually feel more confident in selecting particular conventions in response to the children's interests, which focus their engagement and prompt consideration of the underlying issues. For example, writing or drawing in role can create an atmosphere of individual intent, enabling the teacher to establish a quieter, more reflective mode of operation.

How do I introduce classroom drama to children who have never done it before?

Initially you'll find it useful to ascertain your children's perceptions about drama, ask them what they think it is and what they anticipate having to do. This will reveal their attitudes and help to explain their subsequent behaviour. Talk informally about their ideas and make it clear that drama involves thinking, imagining and understanding, that it involves learning. This explanation is also for their parents, who will certainly hear from their youngsters about drama sessions. Share your commitment and enthusiasm, your expectation that they will enjoy it and learn from it.

Sometimes the contrast with the rest of the curriculum may make children feel that drama isn't work and that it doesn't therefore require work-like behaviour. You will need to state clearly that classroom drama involves thinking and believing, and although it sometimes feels like play it is really work. You will also need to agree some simple rules with the children about stop signals, the working space, the use of materials, and your drama symbol. The drama symbol, which indicates that drama has or is about to begin, should be placed in clear view in the classroom, this will reassure your young learners that although the experience may feel real, it is in fact make believe. This symbol (a stuffed animal or large object) should be out of sight when drama is not happening.

It is important to ensure that all your class finish their first drama session with a sense of achievement, feeling sure they can 'do drama'. Consequently the initial activities need to be easily manageable, for example, making a small group or whole class freeze frame of some narrative action. Allowing friends to work together in this session will ease the negotiation skills required, and your positive feedback at the end of the session will encourage them.

Isn't classroom drama rather noisy?

Drama, the art form of social living, demands discussion and verbal involvement. This can lead to higher than usual noise levels, since a class of children working out how to create their group freeze frames are bound to make more noise than normal. But this does not provide a license for children to make unreasonable or unacceptable noise. Each teacher has their own noise tolerance level and taking into account the nature of each activity, the room being used and the children themselves, teachers need to establish an appropriate working volume. However, if the children are more conscious of the need to keep their noise down than upon engaging in the drama, then the learning outcomes will be limited. Classroom drama often produces humour, heightened engagement and interaction, but it should also produce careful listening and the creation of atmosphere and tension. Excessive noise can work against powerful tension, so a reduction to a working 'hub-ub' will often be necessary, and again a balance of drama conventions will provide for moments of quietness, intensity and even silence.

Do I need a lot of space to work in?

Historically, the traditional view of drama as being sister to the school play, associated with music and movement, meant that the school hall became the normal place for drama. However, there are several disadvantages in using this large space, not the least of which is that the children want to use all of it and initially find it hard to resist the physical impulse to rush around in it and perform! But it does offer considerable freedom of movement and the generation of ideas which accompanies the use of the body.

The classroom is often a viable alternative venue, because you and the class gain a sense of privacy and have immediate access to writing/drawing materials. However there are still classrooms which are too cramped for this kind of activity. So the decision to choose the hall or the classroom has to be taken with regard to your circumstances. It is true, moving the furniture is a chore, but this is offset by the advantages of closeness, and the feeling of security offered by their own class space. In fact the 'clutter' and varied spaces left in the classroom, provide interest and different levels which can be put to good effect within the session. Large amounts of space are not often necessary, and free from the constraints of the hall timetable, teachers can make more of their own choices about when to undertake classroom drama. It can, for example, be integrated into an extended history time or used to investigate a character's past following the literacy hour. The opportunities are endless if the classroom is used and the drama can be tailored to fit the learning agenda, the children and the time available.

How long does a classroom drama session last?

This will depend on the age, experience and maturity of the learners, as well as the issue selected for investigation. Drama integrated into topic work can fire the children's interests and encourage them to research and investigate; it might also involve writing in role, map making, drawing diagrams or designing, all in the service of both drama and other areas of the curriculum. If you plan to use classroom drama for multiple ends, then the time opens up and more can be achieved.

So there is no fixed time span for drama, you will need to remain sensitive to the learning involved, which may result in the session being longer or shorter than you planned. With 5-8 year olds, a session can take between 20 minutes to an hour or over, since the children may be engaged in drama activity for 15 minutes and then in writing in role for 15 minutes, before going back into the drama to resolve the predicament for a further 15 minutes. Much will depend upon their needs, the teaching objectives and learning area and the time realistically available.

What can I do about shy children?

Classroom drama is about the generation of ideas, different imaginative possibilities and their subsequent examination in action, so the skill of presenting or performing is only a part. Your comments and feedback to the class need to highlight this, to honour variety and to affirm the nature of this form of drama. The composition of small groups of children needs to be given careful thought, with a variety of friendship, random and engineered groups established over time to give each child a variety of social contexts to work in. When using self selecting groups, less popular children can be left out so you'll need to move quickly and place them in the group in which they are most likely to be accepted. Mix this strategy with creating the groups yourself, although not all the time.

Less confident children may find pair work supportive and some will need time before they feel secure with this new medium, although it is true that many children, normally quiet in the classroom, find the imaginative context liberating and become more confident and vocal in drama. Teachers, if they have the opportunity of watching a visiting drama teacher, often express surprise that these children volunteer for significant roles or voice their views in whole class improvisations.

However, children should never be pressurized into doing classroom drama. Some self conscious children may fear being watched or mocked and may also be 'bossed' around by more confident peers. These difficulties are not insurmountable and ironically it is often through more drama opportunities, not less, that these very youngsters will gain in confidence. Once their experience of drama has shown them they will not be watched or judged, their initial discomfort frequently eases. Some young learners are also initially tentative about stepping into an imaginary situation, it actually seems very real to them and they expect the magic carpet to really take off! Offer such children a safe role in the drama, as the official photographer of the trip perhaps, or allow them to watch the drama unfold on an imaginary TV screen. This enables them to observe, but still remain part of the drama. Once they realise their friends have returned safely, and this is safe make believe, they are usually keen to journey with them on future occasions.

What can I do about difficult children?

Occasionally a child who hasn't experienced much drama, seeks release in being silly, or 'sends up' their offering, and looks for opportunities to show off and make the class laugh. This is often an indication that they feel insecure in drama and support strategies will need to be offered. Try to find a topic directly related to their concerns and interests or give them a particular role in the drama and seek their advice and counsel. By ensuring they are praised and encouraged for their developing commitment, they will find increasing security in their work.

Other children, who are essentially gregarious or assertive, represent a challenge to the teacher, by offering an almost continuous stream of ideas and suggestions. These children are very useful as 'fall-back' initiators at times, but their constant interjections, however positive, can be difficult to handle in the moment to moment interchange of the drama. Try giving these eager leaders a role alongside you. This provides them with a distinct role to fulfil, but also allows you to oversee their position, and foster their contributions at particular points in the drama. The removal of a child from activity happens no more in drama than in any other lesson, but if you need to do so, ask them to sit quietly somewhere at the edge and not disturb the other children. Through not being fully removed, they can see what they are missing and since drama is highly motivating, these children quickly learn to exert more self-discipline, so they can return to be involved with their friends.

How do I engage the children's feelings?

Subjects which are personally close to everyone are the universal ones of our relationships with others. These invariably arouse feelings of one kind or another, and you will need to watch the effect upon the children to protect them from strong and personally negative feelings. The education of the feelings is vitally important and should be worked upon by the teacher, and doing this through the experience of drama is both legitimate and desirable. You will naturally engage their feelings by being involved yourself and taking the imaginative situation, in which responds to real life issues, seriously.

However, the depth to which you can allow your drama to go and allow a consequent release of feelings, has to be governed by the appreciation that the drama lesson is not an individual counselling session. What you are endeavouring to do is address areas of human experience which are relevant to everyone and deserve investigation, such as addressing disappointment. It is not the task of the drama teacher to become the therapist and set out to arouse strong feelings in a group setting. The surfacing of feelings in drama, expressed through the children's engagement, is one way of recognising the quality of drama, because it is direct evidence of their involvement, but an appropriate balance needs to be found between this kind of realness and the emotional safety of the child.

What about emotionally sensitive issues?

A deep involvement with issues is sought in classroom drama, some of which are of a sensitive nature. Very occasionally, as a result of an associated personal experience, one child may be unable to control strong emotions. This is rare, because in constantly moving in and out of the classroom drama, the children develop a sense of 'this is drama time', and know they have one foot in the reality of the classroom. The very strength of drama is that it engages real feelings and emotions in safe, fictional contexts where these can be genuinely encountered and considered. In this way, children come to learn more about themselves and the real world and explore difficult issues in protected imaginary contexts. Real engagement in the fictional context is sought for all the class, but do be ready to offer strategies such as private writing and drawing, as well as activities which prompt social contact and laughter, to help children handle sensitive issues. Older children are more likely to feel these emotions arriving and may seek to disguise their engagement with behaviour which retreats from the situation, such as turning it all into a joke. Humour and laughter are relaxers and releasers of tension, so they can be usefully employed by both you and the children.

What can I do when there are too many ideas to deal with?

Drama generates many ideas and possibilities which the children are eager to share, for their suggestions shape the drama and in doing so extend their understanding. Frequently, several of their different ideas could be developed and the class may need, with your advice, to decide upon which aspect they wish to take forward. You can make the decision for professional reasons, although with older children prioritising and voting are often employed. Later in the drama you might incorporate their different ideas into some narration and so honour the suggestions which were not taken up. Individuals' views about character motivation and other underlying issues may remain open and will need to be revisited in your reflection phase. In extension work some children may want to return to their earlier ideas to explore them further. In classroom drama, one of your aims is to allow a diversity of ideas to be generated, but it is also necessary to negotiate, and accept collective decisions about actions and the direction of events so that a corporate ownership of what takes place develops. Part of your responsibility, therefore, is to manage a fair distribution of responsibility and leadership as the drama develops.

How can I slow the action down?

Most young children are full of ideas and enthusiasm for life, and in classroom drama this can be tapped. Children enjoy the action and want to rush on to solve the problems and live in the moment. Classroom drama however involves both engagement and reflection, and the teacher will want to help the class consider the implications of their actions, and understand characters' motives, inner feelings and issues. Providing time for reflection is essential throughout classroom drama, as it prompts children to make connections and consider the issues more fully on their drama journeys.

Certain drama conventions are more reflective in nature and can be useful to slow the action down, particularly when the children are losing their concentration or are over excited. When this happens, either use the teacher in role to refocus their attention upon a development, or channel the energy being expressed in excitement into some individual task which draws upon their thinking. This could include writing in role, letters and notes, drawing, and creating maps and diagrams. In mapping out the session try to create a varied pace, with activities which demand quiet stillness, concentration and reflection as well as those which demand energy, action, conversation and movement. So avoid building drama upon action alone (reminiscent of 'action' films) but include the action of intensity and human tension. Try to look at the same incidents from different perspectives and deepen meanings.

CONCLUSION

No two lessons are alike, and in teaching classroom drama more so, because the content of what you are teaching is variable by nature. Added to this are the different personalities in your class, (and you) and everyone's changing moods and outlook. This complexity is not negative: however, it is a challenge for you to understand and use. You are already managing these differences minute by minute, day by day, but they need to be reconsidered in managing your drama.

This resource book with its clear structure and recommended plan of conventions, may imply that there is one way to teach and that the lesson plans are to be implemented as written. However, this was not our intention. The lessons are offered as suggestions and constitute a framework within which you need to make your own decisions as the drama unfolds. Their strength is the inclusion of dramatic and challenging situations, but like any well-prepared meal they ultimately rely upon the cook and the cooking! Your oven may be fiercely hot, or may be easily controlled, whichever, you know your class and you will need to adjust the 'cooking' times accordingly, no one but you can really master that! Adjustment to the conditions, or your particular class with its different individuals, relies upon flexibility and an eye for observing the details of what is going on amongst the children, as well as a sensitivity to them as individuals.

Chapter 16

CLASSROOM DRAMA AND LITERACY TIME

Introduction

Drama is a useful tool for enlivening and invigorating Literacy Time, although the structured nature and explicit time frame of the actual literacy hour set out in the National Literacy Strategy's *Framework for Teaching* (1998) doesn't lend itself to a developing classroom drama. However, various drama conventions can be employed in the hour to feed into shared reading and writing, and objectives can be brought to life through dramatic exploration and imaginative interaction. Improvisation demands children's full involvement and this can energise the study of a text and help the learners engage with the theme or the characters, enriching their understanding in the process. Full classroom drama needs time to unfold and should be given its own curriculum time, separate from literacy focused time, in order for children to become accustomed to the drama experience and gain confidence in using this symbolic art form as a tool for imagining, for thinking and for learning.

Texts being studied in devoted literacy time represent useful resource material for classroom drama. For example, the class could, through drama, co-author a chapter of *The Owl who was Afraid of the Dark*, before they hear Jill Tomlinson's version and study one of her chapters in their designated literacy time. In this way, classroom drama can run alongside the literacy hour and can provide quality material for shared writing. Drama is particularly useful for enriching and investigating longer stories at KS1 or creating other tales in the same genre or with the same theme as a literacy hour text. Many schools, in responding creatively to timetabling, are offering one session a week which is used for creative writing and/or drama. Such provision can (alongside other planned speaking and listening opportunities) encompass NC statutory orders for ATI and develop children's imagination in action, which in turn enriches their creative writing.

Drama conventions employed individually in the hour do draw the learner into the text, extend their involvement and understanding and provide rich improvised material for writing. To capitalize on this short lived drama activity you'll need to help the children connect back to the text, and articulate what they've learnt about the characters, theme or plot through e.g. their role play or hot seating. Without this reflection time, this bridging activity between drama and the text, the value of drama in exploring the text is somewhat reduced. For less confident drama teachers, and children inexperienced in drama, using individual drama conventions in literacy time can be a worthwhile introduction to their potential and develop the children's knowledge about dramatic forms as well as their inferential understanding of the text. There are many conventions which can be used to examine narrative and non-fiction and these are noted in this chapter with examples, mainly from big books, to demonstrate this multi-modal approach. Dramatic activities for independent work in the literacy hour are also briefly noted.

Using Drama Conventions in The Literacy Hour

1   INVESTIGATING STORY STRUCTURE

Sorting, ordering and sequencing events in stories is an important skill, so too is imagining and hypothesizing what might happen next. Both can be developed through the use of drama conventions in the literacy hour.

Freeze frames can be made of narrative events which might occur next in the story being read, this will involve the class in actively predicting and hypothesising alternatives. It could be a whole class freeze frame or involve small groups suggesting different scenarios. Selecting one, this could be brought to life in words and action, and then be recounted in shared writing as the next paragraph/section in the story. Alternatively, when a story has been completed, several freeze frames can be made to show the narrative structure, e.g. simple sequential freeze frames could be made to summarise *This is the Bear and the Scary Night* by Sarah Hayes and titles given to each one. In effect a corporate storyboard of the text is physically made by the children, and by recording the titles of these freeze frames, a resumé of the story is written. This involves reflection, re-visitation and retelling of the main events in the tale. Factual information gathered from a text can also be represented as freeze frames and labelled/titled accordingly.

Orally retelling a tale or part of one in role is another option for revisiting story structure. For example, at the end of *The Train Ride* by June Crebbin, when the little girl arrives at her destination and embraces her grandmother, the teacher could be in role as grandma, and the class as her grandchild. Together, the class can reconstruct her journey and retell the sights seen and places visited. Alternatively, pairs of children could *role play* this reflective conversation about the journey, aided perhaps by the class train track story map. Similarly at the close of *This is the Bear* by Sarah Hayes, the dog could retell the bear's adventures to the other toys in the bedroom, so in small groups, one individual retells the tale, whilst the others ask questions to act as memory prompts.

2   INVESTIGATING CHARACTERS

This is a rich area for dramatic examination in the hour since drama conventions can increase the children's awareness of a character's behaviour, motives, speech and emotions, as well as establish their point of view.

Thought tracking or thinking out loud in role as a character is considerably more demanding than responding to a teacher's questions about how a character feels, and it enables all the children to engage more fully with the character's views. For example, in working on *This is the Bear* by Sarah Hayes and taking up a physical position like the bear who has been left at the dump, the class could listen to a couple of suggestions from the teacher and then simultaneously speak out loud the thoughts and feelings of the lonesome bear. In listening to their own words and voicing the bear's fears, the children and you, will all be involved in being the character, albeit briefly. You could also ask some individuals to voice a few of their thoughts to the class. The eventual class list of words and phrases to describe the bear's state of mind, will be more varied as a consequence of this engagement and is likely to be created by a wider number of children. It may be helpful to challenge the children to group these words under particular emotions, to examine synonyms or to use them in their writing. Thought bubbles can also capture a character's inner feelings which have been generated through the convention of thought tracking.

Hot seating a character provides an opportunity for the class to ask questions and find out more about an individual. For example in *The Rainbow Fish* by Marcus Pfeiffer, the beautiful but vainglorious rainbow fish refuses to share his shiny scales and so loses friends. He cannot understand this. This fish (teacher in role) could be hot seated by the wise octopus or his parents (the class) in order to establish why he is behaving like this, to tease out what others think of him and whether he can be persuaded to change. Following the hot seat, a reflection time needs to summarise what has been learnt about the character. Alternatively, the conversation could be scribed in shared writing as a piece of dialogue.

Role play in pairs or with the whole class and the teacher, can also provide the chance to expand the text and build a sense of the characters through improvising conversations which are not developed in the story. For example, in *Oscar Got the Blame* by Tony Ross, Oscar's mother's response and reprimands could be improvised with Oscar trying to defend himself. Such conversations can be captured in speech bubbles or as dialogue, and examples used to teach sentence or word level objectives.

Decision alley can be used to examine the advantages and disadvantages of situations from a particular character's point of view. For example, in *Where the Wild Things Are* by Maurice Sendak, Max, having sent the wild things to bed, could walk through the forest and decide whether to stay or return home. The class could make a path from two lines of children, and let one child as Max walk slowly down the decision alley, his mind reflecting upon the pros and cons of returning home. When Max reaches the end he can be asked for his decision, what views persuaded him one way or another? Recording these views in two quick lists will help the children perceive the complex nature of decision making and compromise.

Role on the wall can provide insight into a character's thinking, their values, feelings and attitudes. For example, in John Burningham's touching story *Grandpa*, the old man could be drawn in outline as the role on the wall and his own thoughts and fears can be entered into the shape. In re-visiting the text in shared reading, the child's views of her grandfather may be inferred through their various interchanges and recorded outside the role outline, to build up, a richer picture of their relationship. So the character's thoughts are noted inside, and others' views of them recorded outside the outline.

Writing in role as a character in a tale can also help the children explore the thoughts and feelings, perspectives and views of significant individuals. For example, in *Where's My Teddy* by Jez Alborough, Eddie, following a role play in which he tells his mum all about his day in which he lost his teddy and met the 'big bear', could write a diary entry about this day's adventures. This could be scribed by the teacher in shared writing or written individually as first person narrative.

3   INVESTIGATING THEMES

The underlying theme of the text is an interesting area to examine through small group drama work. In this context, the children may more easily share their views and through observing other groups' representations of the theme, alternatives are more fully considered.

Freeze frames (group or class) can usefully summarise various themes in a text. The children can represent the poem or story to show what the literature is exploring or the message the writer might have been trying to convey. For example, in a Year 1 class, the children decided that Martin Waddell had written *Owl Babies* to remind people that '*our mummies love us*' and that '*you must always stay together if you are in trouble*'. Their freeze frames showed the baby owls huddled together on the branch with and without their mothers. Gradually, children become able to create more symbolic freeze frames which are in effect abstract sculptures reflecting the theme of the text. For example, in a Year 2 class, one group of children showed the theme of *Not Now Bernard* by David McKee, with one child sitting on the floor and four others in a square, standing around her and facing outwards. They called this stone sculpture, '*If you're small, you get ignored*'. In discussing the theme and how to represent it in a freeze frame, children become actively involved in learning about the text. Whole class thematic sculptures with the teacher can demonstrate abstract representations and provide models to work from.

Using Drama in Independent Work in the Hour

Drama work in this time will necessarily be short lived, but nonetheless collaborative and imaginative drama activities represent valid independent work tasks related to NLS teaching objectives and children's learning targets. They can help children develop their understanding of structure, character and plot and prompt the children to use a range of spoken language registers and a wide vocabulary. Feedback about these activities to the whole class is essential.

- *Small world play* could involve creating the setting of the tale by drawing pictures and making use of materials to re-play or retell the story with the props. This will reinforce the sense of story structure. Puppets are also invaluable for such work.

- *Role play area re-enactment* could involve remaking the tale in a related role play area, e.g. re-enacting *The Rainbow Fish* by Marcus Pfeiffer in an ocean. The group may elect a narrator or improvise together as they revisit the structure, re-enact the story, and take up roles.

- *Role play area improvisation* could involve improvising a new tale in a role play area which is related to the genre being studied, e.g. if the focus is traditional tales, then a castle or forest would suit. The children can select who they are (people) and their problem (predicament) and then seek to improvise a story based on this. The class could even create a portrait gallery of possible inhabitants or visitors, with a list of possible predicaments. So each group select their own scenario to help shape their improvisation. Such small group improvisational drama would be enriched by the involvement of an adult in role.

- *Taped retellings of a story* could involve a group focusing on the story structure and retelling the whole tale or focusing upon a detailed retelling of a particular incident. Both have dramatic overtones in the small group reconstruction.

- *Improvised conversations or interviews in role* can emerge from fiction or non-fiction content as a precursor to paired writing. Tape recorders or empty speech bubbles on a photocopy of the text can help structure this activity.

CONCLUSION

Drama offers the chance to enliven literacy time through using the children's imagination and developing their affective engagement and personal response. Expanding the repertoire of drama conventions used in the literacy hour and taking opportunities to include drama in this time, can offer both teachers and children increased interactive involvement and satisfaction. Classroom drama itself, however, needs to be given separate curriculum time in order to explore and create texts through more extended and sustained investigation.

Chapter 17
CLASSROOM DRAMA CONVENTIONS

Introduction

A range of drama conventions exist which can be employed in classroom drama. Individually, each creates different demands and prompts particular kinds of thinking and interaction appropriate at particular moments in the drama. To use them effectively, you will need to become well acquainted with these conventions, so this chapter explores the nature and purpose of the major conventions, and provides examples to bring them to life. They are not however rigid structures and can be flexibly adapted. For convenience they are examined in alphabetical order.

Decision Alley

This convention refers to any situation in which there are different choices of action, conflicting interests or dilemmas. It is useful to examine the pros and cons of a decision. Two lines of children face each other, approximately two paces apart and reasonably spaced out. One child in role walks slowly down the alley between them. As the character progresses down the alley, their thoughts or the sets of views for and against a course of action, which the role faces, are voiced out loud by the rest of the class. The character can then be hot seated at the end of the alley, to establish their final decision and to understand why they have made this choice. For example, Little Red Riding Hood's thoughts can be voiced in a decision alley when she considers whether or not to stray from the path in the forest and pick flowers for her grandma.

Drawing in Role

This involves the children individually or in small groups drawing a significant object in the drama. For example, a detailed drawing of the two headed monster seen in an undersea cavern, can help the children flesh out the various features of the creature and sow seeds for future action. In this way the drawing enhances the drama and creates new meanings.

Flashback/Flashforward

This involves the class in exploring some event in a character's past or future, or conjecturing what might be happening simultaneously elsewhere. This device can be equated with the fast forward/rewind on the video player, although the portrayal might be undertaken as a freeze frame or as an improvisation. Flashbacks seek to explain a character's current behaviour, whilst flashforwards seek to examine the consequences of recent events. For example, a flashforward might show a later incident in Miss Muffet's life, when her fear of spiders caused her more intense problems.

Forum Theatre

This is an improvisation performed by a few members of the class in the forum of the classroom, which is then discussed, revisited and developed. In its simplest form with younger children, an important situation is improvised and watched by the class, and the words and actions of those involved are commented upon, (with the helpful mediation of the teacher) and then the same situation is reworked taking into account what has been said. A development of this technique is to offer the children the chance to stop the action, suggest changes and justify their alternative ideas. This convention allows the drama to be revisited, making use of many of their ideas. It is valuable for examining difficult situations more closely and working out how they might best be tackled. For example, in a drama based upon *The Iron Man* by Ted Hughes, the children may have to deal with the scientist who made it, and that interaction could well be tricky for them to negotiate successfully. Using this convention would give them a chance of coaching each other during interchanges in a way which makes the negotiation with the scientist more successful.

Freeze Frame

This convention is also known as creating tableaux, still images or statue making. Individually, in small groups or as a whole class, the children use their bodies to create an image of an event, an idea, a theme or a moment in time. This still silent picture freezes the action, as do newspaper photographs, but freeze frames can also portray a visual memory, or a wish, or show an image from a dream, as well as represent more abstract themes such as anger, jealousy or the truth. For example, in a drama about the voyages of Captain Cook, the children can make freeze frames showing the most unusual creatures he encountered. Freeze frames can also be brought to life, and can be subtitled with an appropriate caption, written or spoken, or have noises and sound effects added to them. Also, the words or inner thoughts of members of the tableau can be voiced when the teacher touches children on the shoulder. Freeze frames offer a useful way of capturing and conveying meaning, since groups can convey much more than they would be able to through words alone.

Group Sculpture

This is closely allied to freeze frame, since the group (or the class) make a sculpture to express a particular aspect of a theme. These tend to be abstract and non-representational in nature and prompt the children to share their own perceptions of key issues in the drama. For example, making a sculpture of one of the themes in *The Jolly Witch* by Dick King Smith.

Hot Seating

In this convention, the teacher and/or the children assume the role of one or more individuals from the drama and are questioned by the remainder of the class. The class need to be forewarned and primed to think of questions. They can ask the questions either as themselves, so their point of view is outside the drama, or they can adopt a role within the drama and ask questions from this perspective. If the class is in role, this helps to focus the kind of questions asked and may prompt the need for notes to be taken. For example, in a drama about stealing and trust, the Knave of Hearts could be questioned about his taking of the tarts, by members of the court. Several characters from the drama can be placed on the hot seat at once, or alternatively a single character on the hot seat can be represented by two or more children, this provides security for whoever is on the hot seat. It is a useful probing technique which seeks to develop knowledge of the character's motives, attitudes and behaviour. It encourages increased reflective awareness of the complex nature of human behaviour.

Improvisation: small group

Improvisation can be spontaneously developed or prepared beforehand. Small groups of children can discuss, plan and then create a piece of prepared improvisation. This kind of improvisation is relatively secure, because through their discussion they create a kind of script or structure to follow. Alternatively, the dramatic scene can be spontaneously improvised by the group, who make it up as they speak and respond to one another in role. For example, in a drama about the environment, in which a monster is laying waste the countryside, groups can be asked to spontaneously improvise the children trying to persuade their parents that this monster really does exist. This requires more confidence but is more rewarding because it reflects actual living and the communicative demands which are faced second by second. It also provides access to children's unconscious preoccupations which are invaluable to the teacher. Some groups of learners hold back from spontaneous improvisation whilst others pitch straight into role; all children need the opportunity to experience both kinds.

Improvisation: whole class

The whole class (including the teacher) engage in improvisation together. Again such improvisation can be planned or spontaneous. It can be formal as in a whole class meeting, for example, a tribal council discussing the misdemeanours of one of its members, or more informal, for example, an improvisation of a scene at the seaside. Whole class role play reduces the pressure of being watched since everyone is corporately engaged and lives in the moment responding to each other naturally in the imaginary context. The teacher in role frequently takes a critical role in whole class improvisation.

Mantle of the Expert

This convention involves children being given roles which necessarily include the expertise, authority, knowledge and skills of specialists. Their expertise is explicitly used in the drama. This knowledge may be recently acquired from classroom research, or it might be their own personal expertise, but the status it gives the children allows them to significantly influence the drama. The teacher must honour their expertise and may therefore take on a role of relative ignorance in the drama, or assume a more equal role alongside them. This general technique, developed by Dorothy Heathcote, is very empowering for young learners, since considerable responsibility is given to the group and insight can be gained into different occupations. For example, establishing a toy museum for children, including not only the exhibits but designing the building and marketing the museum, relies upon their explicit knowledge of museums and toys, as well as their implicit knowledge of children, and it uses their ideas and opinions about display and promotion.

Maps/Diagrams

Together the class make a large collective map or diagram of an area, or the scene of a crime. This can help establish a corporate sense of place, and provides a concrete reference for the events which take place there. Alternatively, groups can produce small maps or diagrams to show more detail about the context. Such visuals often move the drama on, as possible elements are identified through the drawing, and their place in the unfolding events are examined or retained for later use. For example, drawing a map of the castle and its surroundings allows many possibilities related to place, character and incident to be imagined.

Mime

This convention ranges from simple whole class mime in which each child mimes the relevant actions supported by their teacher/narrator, to more refined small group mime and the crafted use of gesture, facial expression and body movement. It is useful to establish an imaginary context and does remove the pressure of dialogue, although in a moment of stillness the teacher can prompt the sharing of the mimed character's inner thoughts by asking them to speak their thoughts out loud. The teacher should stress the need for concentration and care which encourages reflection whilst miming. For example, in searching a slumbering giant's room for a key he has stolen, the teacher in role can demand careful deliberation and remind the class in urgent whispers that they must look in every nook and cranny, but mustn't make a noise.

Narration

This convention relates to the teacher or children as storytellers. In the former, the teacher offers occasional narrative links or a running commentary, for example in an undersea drama the teacher might voice alternative viewpoints about the threat from the sharks. In the latter, child narrators can describe a mime, adding atmosphere and description to the scene created.

Objects

Objects can be useful in drama as they imply actions, events and people, as well as extend meanings which are being built up by the teacher. Through symbolising attitudes, values and relationships they can help establish a character's role and subtly state information about them which is not easily said in words. For example, the arrival of a man at a farm who is carrying a heavy axe or knife and wishes to buy animals, implies that his intentions towards those animals are probably those of a butcher. Such objects operate as wordless metaphors.

Overheard Conversations

In small groups, conversations between characters are improvised and then a few are 'overheard' by the class, to enable a range of viewpoints to be established. The teacher as storyteller may integrate these perspectives into the drama. For example, in a drama about a misguided Maharajah, based upon *The Dancing Tigers* by Russell Hoban, some servants who have been locked into a room might whisper together about their predicament. Their ideas, views and worries could be overheard. Such conversations can add both tension and secrecy to a situation.

Play Making

Using this convention, small groups plan, practice and present extremely short improvisations which might be flashbacks or flashforwards in the life of a character in the community or might express alternative courses of action in the present. This is useful for sequencing ideas and developing confidence in performance. For example, groups might make a brief playlet based upon *The Selfish Giant* by Oscar Wilde, showing what happened when the giant heard the children playing in the garden.

Ritual or Ceremony

In ritual, the teacher and the class together work out ways of marking significant events in the narrative and create some form of ceremony which is part of the drama. Such rituals often slow the drama down and provoke a deepening sense of significance, as well as reflection. For example, the children as villagers might create a song, a dance or even special food in preparation for the Festival of the Moon, or in another drama, different villagers might write prayers and make artefacts to leave at the burial site of their shaman. Ritual is often used to conclude work, or to intensify the tenor of the drama.

Role on the Wall

In this convention, an outline is drawn around a character as they lie upon a large piece of paper, and then information and feelings about the character are written into the shape by each child. This can be added to throughout the drama. It can also be enriched by being written from different perspectives, for example, the space outside the outline can contain comments about the character as they are seen from an observer's viewpoint and the interior space can contain the character's own thoughts and point of view. For example, in exploring the Emperor's character in *The Emperor's New Clothes*, by Hans Christian Andersen, different people's perspectives can be recorded in order to build a deeper understanding of how others viewed him as well as his own views and self perception.

Sound Tracking/Collage

This convention involves sounds being made, via the voice, body or through percussion to evoke atmosphere and express meaning in a musical collage. The sounds can stand alone or be made to accompany action or a freeze frame: either way they encourage children to experiment and convey mood expressively. For example, sailors land on an island and as night falls strange and unusual noises come to their ears; in small groups the children create the eerie noises and then share them with the class. Alternatively the whole class could create the cacophony of sounds together to create atmosphere.

Teacher as Storyteller

This convention involves the teacher using narration to provide structure and coherence, to link action, mark the passage of time or reflect upon a character's perspective and deepen the significance and meaning of events. The teacher can, through careful narration, build atmosphere, change the pace and give form and shape to the dramatic activity. If the tale is told and retold as a drama unfolds, then the teacher can include the children's ideas as part of the narrative. This is significant as it honours their ideas and ensures *their* story is told. This device can be used throughout the drama or just at a few significant moments to introduce, to link or conclude the drama. It is a particularly useful tool in drama sessions with young children.

Teacher in Role

This is the most powerful convention the teacher has at their disposal. It involves the teacher engaging fully in the drama by taking various roles. This technique is a tool through which the teacher can support, extend and challenge the children's thinking from inside the drama. The teacher in role can influence events from within the developing situation. Every role has its own social status which gives access to an influence commensurate with its position. High status roles have a controlling and deciding nature, whilst lower status roles are not so openly powerful but can still be influential. For example, a high status role would be a King or the owner of the shop, whilst a lower status role would be a pageboy at the king's court or a customer. For teachers beginning to use this technique, it is helpful to forewarn the class that you are going into role, and then pause a while before beginning. Whilst in role try not to lose your concentration or come out of role: if you do, they will too. Children value their teacher's commitment and reciprocate in kind.

Telephone Conversations

This involves the children in pairs, improvising the conversation between two characters on the phone at a certain point in the drama. Alternatively, the teacher in role can hold a one way telephone conversation on an imaginary telephone and prompt the class to infer the other half of the conversation. It is a useful device for passing on important information, for letting time pass, for recollecting events and for adding tension to situations. For example, in setting up a bakery shop, the teacher can receive a call from a local hygiene office, informing the workers there will be an inspection in half an hour!

Thought Tracking

In this convention, the private thoughts of individuals are shared publicly. This can be organised in different ways; the teacher can touch individuals on the shoulder during a freeze frame or small improvisation and ask them to voice their thoughts, or the whole class can take on the persona of one individual and simultaneously speak out loud their thoughts and fears in a particular situation. Alternatively, the teacher or child in role, can give witness to the class and speak personally about recent events from a 'special' chair, or members of the class can take turns in moving forward to stand behind the chair and express their thoughts about the character. For example, in a drama in which the central character has been turned to stone by a wizard, the class could make a circle around an empty chair, or a motionless child, and take it in turns to come forward to touch the stone child and express their inner thoughts and fears aloud. This convention is useful to slow down the action and can prompt both a deeper understanding of individual characters and allow a sensitive response to what has happened.

Word Play/Choral Chanting

This is useful to add mood and evoke atmosphere. It involves the children in creating word patterns, phrases or chants which can be repeated or intoned within the drama. For example, in a drama about a giant preying upon a village the children could, in groups, make up a few phrases which the villagers could repeat together as they go about their work, or freeze frames of the giant could be made and a chant devised which emphasises his power or intentions. Such work is often poetic in nature and evocative of different perspectives. Alternatively, the teacher could offer a few lines from a poem, which can be repeated in order to intensify a theme in the drama.

Writing in Role

A variety of kinds of writing can emerge from imagined experience and can be written in role, e.g. letters, postcards, diaries, notes, even graffitti. Young children often write with considerable urgency in drama since they have a purpose and a clearly imagined audience for their writing. For example, in a 'Watership Down' drama the children could write to the rabbits in the next warren to say goodbye and explain why they are leaving. After the close of the drama, writing alongside role may take place when, from a distance outside the drama, newspaper accounts, pamphlets, letters and thank you cards may be written.

CONCLUSION

No drama conventions are fixed and unchangeable, you'll find you can change them to suit your purposes, adapting them to the needs of the drama, and if you create new ones for yourself so much the better. They are not rules. Some conventions have in-built opportunities for performance, which need to be used cautiously, particularly small group improvisation. If you are not careful a great deal of valuable time can be taken up with groups preparing playlets, and then sitting and watching one another. A small amount of this is occasionally justified, but the watching becomes far more valuable if it is purposefully used in the context of the classroom drama, as it is for example in forum theatre. Drama conventions help shape the meaning and need to be employed appropriately to open up the imaginary world, create the characters and investigate the issues within the unfolding narrative.

Further Reading

If you would like to read more about teaching drama, we recommend the following books which discuss both theory and practice.

Booth, D. (1994) *Storydrama: Reading, Writing and Role Playing Across the Curriculum*, Ontario, Pembroke.

Davies, G. (1983) *Practical Primary Drama*, Oxford, Heinemann.

Heathcote, D. and Bolton, G. (1995) *Drama for Learning*, Portsmouth, Heinemann.

Kitson, N. and Spiby, I. (1997) *Drama 7-11: Developing Primary Teaching Skills*, London, Routledge.

Neelands, J. (1984) *Making Sense of Drama*, Oxford, Heinemann.

Neelands, J. (1992) *Learning through Imagined Experience*, Sevenoaks, Hodder and Stoughton.

O'Neill, C. (1995) *Drama Worlds: A Framework for Process Drama*, Portsmouth, Heinemann.

Readman, G. and Lamont, G. (1994) *Drama: A Handbook for Primary Teachers*, London, BBC.

Taylor, K. (ed) (1991) *Drama Strategies: New Ideas from London Drama*, Oxford, Heinemann.

Winston, J. and Tandy, M. (1998) *Beginning Drama 4-11,* London, David Fulton.

thinking
and
reflecting